T0312284

Cambridge Elements ≡

Elements in International Relations
edited by
Jon C. W. Pevehouse
The University of Wisconsin–Madison
Tanja A. Börzel
Freie Universität Berlin
Edward D. Mansfield
University of Pennsylvania
Associate Editors
Sarah Kreps
Cornell University
Anna Leander
Graduate Institute Geneva

PEACE IN DIGITAL INTERNATIONAL RELATIONS

Prospects and Limitations

Oliver P. Richmond
University of Manchester

Gëzim Visoka
Dublin City University

Ioannis Tellidis
Kyung Hee University

CAMBRIDGE
UNIVERSITY PRESS

CAMBRIDGE
UNIVERSITY PRESS

Shaftesbury Road, Cambridge CB2 8EA, United Kingdom

One Liberty Plaza, 20th Floor, New York, NY 10006, USA

477 Williamstown Road, Port Melbourne, VIC 3207, Australia

314–321, 3rd Floor, Plot 3, Splendor Forum, Jasola District Centre,
New Delhi – 110025, India

103 Penang Road, #05–06/07, Visioncrest Commercial, Singapore 238467

Cambridge University Press is part of Cambridge University Press & Assessment,
a department of the University of Cambridge.

We share the University's mission to contribute to society through the pursuit of
education, learning and research at the highest international levels of excellence.

www.cambridge.org
Information on this title: www.cambridge.org/9781009396745

DOI: 10.1017/9781009396752

First published 2023

A catalogue record for this publication is available from the British Library.

ISBN 978-1-009-39674-5 Paperback
ISSN 2515-706X (online)
ISSN 2515-7302 (print)

Cambridge University Press & Assessment has no responsibility for the persistence
or accuracy of URLs for external or third-party internet websites referred to in this
publication and does not guarantee that any content on such websites is, or will
remain, accurate or appropriate.

Peace in Digital International Relations

Prospects and Limitations

Elements in International Relations

DOI: 10.1017/9781009396752
First published online: March 2023

Oliver P. Richmond
The University of Manchester

Gëzim Visoka
Dublin City University

Ioannis Tellidis
Kyung Hee University

Author for correspondence: Oliver P. Richmond, oliver.richmond
@manchester.ac.uk

Abstract: The international architecture of peacebuilding and statebuilding is currently responding to a shift from 'analogue' to 'digital' approaches in international relations. This is affecting conflict management, intervention, peacebuilding, and the all-important role of civil society. This Element analyses the potential that these new digital forms of international relations offer for the reform of peace praxis – namely, the enhancement of critical agency across networks and scales, the expansion of claims for rights and the mitigation of obstacles posed by sovereignty, locality, and territoriality. The Element also addresses the parallel limitations of digital technologies in terms of political emancipation related to subaltern claims, the risk of co-optation by historical and analogue power structures, institutions, and actors. The authors conclude that though aspects of emerging digital approaches to making peace are promising, they cannot yet bypass or resolve older, analogue conflict dynamics revolving around power relations, territorialism, and state formation

Keywords: digital peace, analogue politics, digital technologies, international relations, peacebuilding

ISBNs: 9781009396745 (PB), 9781009396752 (OC)
ISSNs: 2515-706X (online), 2515-7302 (print)

Contents

1 Introduction

As with many areas of scientific endeavour, intellectual and policy attempts to make peace after war have recently been enthused by the implications of new data-driven, remote, and even automated possibilities and technologies.[1] This Element intends to explore and outline the prospective debates about peace and peacemaking in the new digital frameworks emerging in International Relations (IR).[2] It offers a critical evaluation of the digitalization of peace efforts in the context of changing trends of war and violence.

From a practical perspective, exploiting innovations related to the emergence of new capacities and technologies, networks, and communications, makes strategic and tactical sense for peacemaking, peacekeeping, peacebuilding, and for civil society approaches.[3] However, through a critical lens some such 'innovations' appear to be displacement activities, whilst some are contradictory in that they offer advantages and disadvantages simultaneously. This study intends to explore these tensions from the perspective of the evolving concept of peace and its place in IR. This is necessary because international relations are increasingly marked by a distinction between 'analogue' (characterized as intensely geopolitical, elite-oriented, and power-based, operating in standard time, and dependent on human capacities and knowledge) modes of statecraft, diplomacy, and military action, and new 'digital' innovations (which are connected to new technologies and their powerful owners, marked by speed, remoteness, lessened risk, and enormous datasets).

New technologies of war and violence have marked conflicts from Iraq and Afghanistan to Syria and Yemen, as well as impacting on, or destabilizing, peace agreements and supposedly peaceful states such as Colombia or Brazil. There is also a strong argument that they have led to 'backsliding' in established democracies such as the United States and United Kingdom (Haggard and Kaufman 2021). In cases such as Israel-Palestine and Afghanistan, the viability of a victor's peace – and its collapse – seems to be seen by foreign policy elites (though not by multilateral actors) as plausible when supported by new

---

[1] For the UN's interest in this new area, see for example, https://futuringpeace.org/, https://dppa.un.org/en/innovation.

[2] This Element partially draws on the following papers: Richmond 2020; Richmond and Tellidis 2020; Richmond and Visoka 2021a. See also: Howard 2015; Owen 2015; Monshipouri 2016; Chandler 2018; *The Economist* 2018; Zuboff 2019b.

[3] This study focuses on the range of different tools that are used to make peace, including peacebuilding which has come to be seen to be a generic term incorporating a wide range of earlier approaches, including peacekeeping, mediation, diplomacy, state reform, statebuilding, stabilization, regional and international security, and development. However, we recognize the nuances across these tools, and that peacebuilding has never really proven to be an adequate conceptual umbrella.

technologies of war, diplomacy, information, and media associated with great power interests and norms.[4]

Data-driven, remote, automated capacities, operating at scale and speed over great distances, have disrupted power relations and traditional political and military affairs (part of what was referred to as a 'revolution in military affairs' previously) (Der Derian 2019). They have favoured innovation in geopolitics, perhaps also in related diplomatic practice and authoritarian power rather than in peacemaking. Ultimately, this points to the need to think more deeply about peacemaking in a multipolar, high-tech form of international relations, as opposed to the recent analogue and multilateral past. Either way, any developments in IR that lead to new forms of war, and new tensions, need to be responded to with reformed peacemaking systems and architectures (Hinsley 1963; Richmond 2022). These substantial developments have affected international activity, government, and the social actors in different wars, large or small, as well as in authoritarian, developing, and fragile states. So far outcomes have been overwhelmingly negative for conflict-affected populations and for peace processes (the collapse of democracy and peacebuilding in Afghanistan and the war in Ukraine in 2022 (Monten 2014; Allan 2020) being the latest examples), and at best have failed to live up to the early promise that new technologies and possibilities would enhance the emancipatory capacities of peace.

The evolution of 'digital peace' systems, as with other peace innovations in the constantly changing history of war, has lagged behind the evolution of violence in digital international relations (Owen 2015; Monshipouri 2016). This is of serious concern because historically a failure to respond to technological innovation pertaining to violence and war has led to systemic collapse, with subsequent recovery through innovative peace praxis following much later (but normally too late to be preventative or to stop the tragic consequences or war) (Tainter 1988). So far digital enhancements in peacebuilding, peacekeeping, and peacemaking seem to be both ambitious in practical terms and also, from a more critical perspective, represent a reduced ethical ambition. What is certain is that they have undermined human security, rights and democratization processes (see UN Security Council 2021).

New Contributions to Peace in IR

After recent failures in peacemaking, and lengthy wars since 9/11 from Afghanistan and Iraq to Syria and Yemen, it was always likely that new

---

[4] See the debacle of the US withdrawal from Afghanistan in 2021, or former US president Trump's peace deal for the Israel/Palestine in 2020.

approaches to peacemaking would emerge. However, many of them are optimistic, not born out of evidence, and may have unintended consequences. There have been claims that digital peace approaches (Guo et al. 2018; Gleditsch 2019) might offer some promise in overcoming the problems, spoilers, and blockages (Stedman 1997; Richmond and Pogodda 2016) that liberal peace has faced to date. This is despite the fact that such digital possibilities are elite-led, top-down, and speculative due to their connection to what has become known as 'surveillance capitalism' (Zuboff 2019b). Digital advances such as those related to expanding the inclusion of different actors and networks in peace processes, the facilitation of dialogue, back channels, and so social reconciliation, as well as countering various threats, the bridging of distance, failed infrastructure, and the provision of better knowledge or intelligence (Larrauri and Kahl 2013) have been small in scale, even if promising for civil society and their global networks in particular (Kaldor 2003).

Such potentially significant innovations, however, raise the old question of whether small-scale improvements in peacemaking address past political deficits often related to power relations and justice or sustainability issues, or merely represent attempts at pacification – a form of digital counter-insurgency on behalf of hegemons increasingly developing new technologies of power (Foucault 1995). They have proven far from being aligned with the massive disruptions that have occurred in broader international relations. In the past such disruptions, as in the Industrial Revolution, presaged new types of war, such as industrial or total war. These subsequently led to new approaches to peace, such as arose with the UN Charter, but these always lagged behind developments in war-making (Richmond 2022).

Debates and practices have moved forward since early discussions, however. In response to ethnic, secessionist, sectarian, hybrid, and other forms of civil war, information and communication technologies (ICTs) have shown limited potential in the contexts of humanitarian relief, development, early warning systems, the prevention and/or monitoring of pre- and post-electoral violence, and the use of big data for peacekeeping (Tellidis and Kappler 2016; McCarthy 2017; Merrin 2019). There is, however, wide diversity of digital technologies that might be claimed to be useful for the purposes of supporting existing practices of peacemaking, peace-building, statebuilding, stabilization, development, and humanitarianism. They might plausibly contribute to better, more positive forms of peace, accessible to a variety of developers and users, and their interest in deploying these tools means that each of these technologies navigates and interacts with the spaces (virtual and analogue alike), the dynamics, and the asymmetries of conflict.

Clearly, however, their impact is little understood, but the question remains as to whether peace may be substantively improved in critical terms. Do they lead to better political outcomes that address justice and reconciliation issues as well as security and stability problems? As the literature on peacemaking has moved through various iterations, from the victor's peace and the balance of power, to liberal, hybrid, everyday, spatial, emancipatory, and many other iterations that bring peace and justice into a closer relationship with each, it has converged on issues of human security, justice, relative equality, recognition, and sustainability (UN General Assembly 2016; UN Security Council 2016; UN 2018). This provides a critical framework for trying to understand digital potential for peacemaking in the discussion that follows in the rest of this Element.

Digital Contributions

Digital technologies have been relevant in analysing conflict dynamics using social media, big data, text mining programmes, machine learning, digital maps and/or a combination of some or all of the above. Digital communication tools have expanded the inclusion and enhanced strategic communication with all conflict parties and affected population. Some of the aforementioned tools empower local, national, and international peace actors to respond in real time, while others offer an opportunity for enhanced analysis and comprehensive guidance. Digital technologies are increasingly being used to change the dynamics of negotiation after a fully fledged civil war, to handle negotiations in the context of electoral violence, and to design national dialogue processes after a popular uprising or local insurgency (Hirblinger 2020).

When this potential is regarded as small scale, immediate, and separate from political reform and wider ethico-political as well as scientific requirements, it appears more significant. In longer-term processes, new technologies such as digital and virtual platforms are also being used to bridge cultural and ethnic divides by invalidating and refuting exclusionary discourses and re-establishing the basis for cooperation, legitimacy, and shared political narratives. The significance of these new technologies has duly been noted by the UN, which is now increasingly seeking to benefit from their use both for the longer-term design and execution of its peace missions as well as for the satisfaction of the shorter-term needs of those affected by conflict and violent crises (Richmond 2020; Richmond and Tellidis 2020; UN 2021).

It is not the aim of this Element to offer a detailed examination and evaluation of each of these technologies, however. Rather than disaggregating the 'digital' in relation to peace, our objective is to highlight both the emancipatory and alienating potential inherent in the various theoretical and practical approaches that are emerging. The analysis is thus oriented towards a particular focus on the opportunities, challenges, and risks that the digital realm of IR and war and peace therein poses for the international architecture of peacebuilding and statebuilding in the twenty-first century (Richmond 2021). It focuses on the most pressing areas and issues within this thematic and the broader area of digital IR, thus exploring and contributing to a new debate and mapping a new agenda. It has become clear that this task requires synthesized, cross-pollinated research on the much-heralded digital developments in IR and peacebuilding theory and practice, and responses to the changing dynamics of war and conflict in IR. In doing so, the study explores both the innovative aspects that digital technologies have brought to peacebuilding efforts, while also highlighting the tensions, dilemmas, and risks associated with such novel approaches (Hirblinger 2020).

This enables an evaluation of the extent to which technological innovations can 'revolutionize' the international and domestic politics of peacekeeping, mediation, conflict transformation, liberal peacebuilding, and statebuilding paradigms. Might digital technologies restore some of the legitimacy that was lost due to the clashes of ideology, geopolitical and economic interests, and/or a decline of political will to initiate and sustain positive conflict transformation? The empirical sections of the Element critically evaluate various cases of new technologies as used by the UN in conflict-affected settings, as well as other significant international actors (states, but also donor organizations), non-governmental organizations (NGO), civil society organizations and citizens' initiatives to highlight and evaluate the political implications of such new possibilities for peacemaking (Owen 2015). That is, it is necessary to understand how peace is to be made in an emerging and evolving digital system of international relations, and what its qualities might be, in particular, for the impact upon bottom-up and hybrid dynamics of peace formation (Richmond 2016).

Key themes examined in relation to these goals relate to the changing nature of war and violence in an increasingly relational, networked, and digital IR, where states remain dominant actors but are also subject to increasing economic, political, social, and technological pressures. Similarly, the systems of international peacemaking and the development of civil society networks face huge intellectual and practice challenges. Consequently, we examine questions relating to:

- the dysfunctionality of the liberal peace and whether digital, more participatory forms of peace efforts can alter, or possibly hybridize its problematic character;
- the conceptualization of peace architecture and its critical evaluation; the relationship between intervention and peacebuilding, in their analogue and digital forms;

- the potential of digital technologies to overcome the flaws of analogue peacebuilding, especially how increased direct participation (emanating from the very nature of new technologies) could promote more a locally legitimate basis for peace, including the ramifications this has for the legitimacy of the international architecture of peace (IPA); and
- the risks that the 'digitalization' of peace efforts might be co-opted and controlled by hegemonic powers (much like analogue forms of peace efforts have been).

Ambivalent Dynamics

The amalgamation of peacebuilding efforts with new digital technologies represents an important but ambivalent turn in global and local efforts for ending wars and building peace. The adaptation of new digital technologies for peacebuilding has partly taken place as a response to emerging problems in the IPA in order to overcome blockages (Pogodda et al. 2022). In this context, digital technologies may provide new emancipatory scope to bypass peace-capturing dynamics. Peacebuilding actors are exploring digital political and international dynamics and tools partially in response to the inadequacies of peacekeeping, mediation, peacebuilding, and statebuilding in recent times. There has been an expectation that this might ensure that programmes and interventions are designed in such a way as to maximise their effectiveness and legitimacy in conflict-affected societies. Yet, digital contributions have little scope for shaping political agendas or the direction that digital technologies take (a form of digital governmentality, in other words) (Badouard et al. 2016; Richmond 2020), which risks sidelining emancipatory forms of peacebuilding and peace in response to unmet political claims as a concept.

There is no doubt that digital technologies might enhance peacebuilding efforts if they are taken to resolve around concepts like negative peace, resilience, and everyday dynamics solely, but it is important to also account for the structural risks that new digital technologies for peace can have for many conflict-affected societies, partly because they are connected to military, intelligence, state and elite level, media, and other political and economic power structures. While they offer the augmentation of civil society, multilateral structures, and global rights frameworks, evidence also indicates how easily these are disrupted.

Thus, new digital technologies should be treated as a somewhat ambiguous supplement to, rather than a replacement of existing practices in the states-system and global political economy (Richmond and Visoka 2021a, 2021b). This is because they offer the temptation – through the capacity for remote operation, their connection with existing power structures, and residual bias in data patterns and algorithms – of governing risk and war from afar without endangering vital interests in the older, extant geopolitical systems (themselves driven by geopolitics, *realpolitik*, and extraction). The challenge of digital peacebuilding is how to utilize new technologies for social and political emancipation without falling into the traps and distractions that such externally controlled platforms can impose on peacemaking and peacebuilding endeavours.

For the most part, digital technologies, social media platforms, and other ICTs used for peacemaking are useful to, and engaged with, by interlocutors in conflict-affected societies. Yet, that does not mean that social, political, and economic life has entirely embraced the digital domain. Thus, it is important to think through how to tailor the use of digital technologies to the local context and absorption capacities, bearing in mind that global elites and powerful actors tend to do such tailoring with all of the issues this raises. In many conflict-affected settings, analogue politics and networks related to the residual rationalities of state and empire, and territorial sovereignty, tend to dominate the design of institutions, social life, and economic affairs: a legacy of early eras and rationalities. So, it is crucial to explore what it means to pursue peace through digital approaches in an environment that is still analogue in countries shattered by violent conflict (i.e. peacemaking and politics are thus rooted in different rationalities of politics). How suitable are digital peace technologies for resolving contemporary conflicts?

There is clearly a risk that a significant number of advanced digital technologies are not aligned with the social and political realities of conflict-affected societies, given how they have emerged. Political time and space are not clearly harmonized with digital peace. Societies affected by violent conflict have deeply rooted tension concerning a broad range of issues, mostly of an analogue nature. While digital technologies might well overcome certain blockages to peacemaking set by counter-peace forces (Pogodda et al. 2022), it is important to highlight that for peace to receive social legitimacy it needs to relate to the needs of affected communities and must enable them to have the possibility to shape the contours of such a peace process.

Contrary to this assumption, which is common to much peacemaking literature, digital peace approaches may tend to distance politics from local claims and needs, while giving an impression of agency and cooperation, risking thus the production of new forms of alienation and exclusion. In this regard, when not fit for specific contexts, digital technologies connected to peace operations may indirectly support a regressive push away from effort to localize and optimize peacemaking to the local needs and political agencies.

Thus, unbalanced and externally induced efforts to push for digital peace might be prone to failure due to an asynchronous relationship with the existing analogue approaches to peace.

In other words, conflict prevention, transformation, and resolution require a lot more than extended reach, reactive speed or surveillance, reduced risk, covert presence, predictive politics, and artificial intelligence. There is no substitute for political will when it comes to engaging substantively and materially with political and justice claims in conflict-affected societies. According to long-standing and broad scientific evidence, which should not be ignored on the grounds of the emergence of experimental, mitigating approaches (a neoliberal argument about resilience in other words) (Chandler 2014), peacemaking depends on using political rather than technical solutions to address the root causes of war and violence. Such roots are often shaped by elite or external political and geopolitical interests – and can only be dealt with by developing strategies for representation, restitution, reconciliation, justice, and the production of sustainable and emancipatory, alternative political orders.

Structure of the Element

Our critical examination (Koopman 2013, 48) analyses the relationship between conflict and peace problems and policy solutions under digital conditions, given these differ significantly from previous historical contexts across a wide range of dynamics (Visoka 2019). The first section examines the transition from analogue to digital IR and focuses on exploring the dynamics that have determined such a transition and the implications for peace, security, and order. Section 2 looks at peace in analogue international relations, which were characterized by territorially sovereign states, and twentieth-century politics and technology, moderated by the national interest and limited international cooperation, which protected long-standing hierarchies. Section 3 looks at the intersection between peace and new digital technologies in world politics, in which IR, peace, security, and order are no longer centred on the territorial state, but on an amorphous, complex, and unstable set of networks, with constantly changing personal, fluid goals, all dependent upon the next technological enhancement, which shifts their capacities again.

The second part of this study focuses on the promise and limitations of a potential digital turn in peace and conflict studies, namely for efforts to build sustainable peace in conflict-affected societies. Section 4 looks at the promise of technology in complementing existing efforts for peacebuilding. A potential 'revolution in peacebuilding affairs' (Richmond 2014; Pogodda 2020) in the digital sphere seeks to compensate for the current lack of direct and indirect access for the UN, various internationals, donors, leading states, and international non-governmental organizations (INGO), in the world's conflict, emergency, revolutionary, and development areas. In Section 5, we turn to explore the dilemmas and limits of digital peacebuilding. We argue that digital peacebuilding is still embryonic, lacks emancipatory goals connected to subaltern political claims, and without legal and ethical regulation it risks becoming a form of digital governmentality harnessed by political hegemony and geopolitics. The Element concludes with a summary of the pros and cons of the digitalization of peace in IR and its impact on the existing transitional international order. Section 6 provides an overview of the directions and backsliding that a digital turn in peacebuilding practices is likely to take.

2 Peace in Analogue International Relations

Introduction

The 'analogue' framework for various conceptualizations has become an important reference point describing the old, industrial (and pre-industrial) non-digital, and offline technologies and methods of communication and technology across a range of disciplines. It has often been used to highlight its potential and limitations, which is significant for the evolution and potential of political community, the nature of the state, the workings of the international system, and political economy. Ultimately, it made global governance more plausible in the twentieth century, created the potential for more multilateral, economic, civil, and social networks with more political capacity than ever, as well as increased the political awareness of global populations. It has implications for norms and standards in international relations, very relevant to how the concept of peace has been understood and has developed, as well as for self-determination, human rights, development, and democracy. This section examines what this framework means for how we understand peace in international relations.

Conceptualizing the Analogue

The analogue concept is polymorphous. Its meaning has changed over time and mostly in comparison to the conceptualization of the concept of the digital, which is supposed to offer a marked change in the way technology frames the political potential of the current era. In its most recent iterations, the *Oxford English Dictionary* defines analogue as 'a person or thing seen as comparable to another'. It tends to describe things and tools which have a continuous, direct association with the world (Wilden 1980, 156). The concept of the analogue tends to represent a broad spectrum of domains that are human-scaled, relatable, temporal-spatial, formal, and relatively fixed.

In the analogue world, the human was at the centre of processing and interpreting computational data. For the most part, the analogue tends to imitate nature. Hassan argues that 'analogue technologies were technologies whose actions upon the world were actions that we could recognize because they were analogous to the process in nature' (Hassan 2018, 2546). As opposed to the analogue world, 'digital logic has no recognizable analogue in nature; neither is it human-centred or human-scaled' (Hassan 2018, 7). The analogue is also associated with the 'seamless and inviolable veracity of space and time ... connoting something authentic and natural, against the artificial, arbitrarily truncated precision of the digital' (Robinson 2008, 21). It is mediated by humans, even if their capacities are augmented by industrial technologies, which simply extend previous capacities but do not intervene in their mediation. For example, an international conference was possibly very similar in the nineteenth century to one in the twentieth century, except in terms of its logistics and the amount of time that went into organizing it. Analogue capacities in IR have been an accelerant for processes in IR, extending their scale and possibilities, but have had limited impact in mediating IR.

While the analogue is often associated with the non-digital, 'the entire world outside of digital processing is not analog [*sic*], because analog represents a particular technocultural relationship to nature' (Sterne 2016, 32). Moreover, the analogue is not an antithesis of technology. The twentieth century was dominated by analogue computers and technologies which paved the foundations for the transition to digital technologies. During the analogue era, the function of digital computers and technology in general was to improve the performance of defence systems which then gradually spread into business culture and society. While digital domains are slightly different when it comes to the non-material manifestation of thinking, acting, and being in the world, they tend to mimic the spatial experiences and expectations. In this sense, the analogue is embedded in the digital domains through the principle of dimensionality, relatability, and continuity. In other words, digital technologies, including computer interface designs and various applications, tend to share similar ontological features that have long been practised in the analogue world. Reading digital data or content (numbers, text, or image) is an 'analog process' because 'outside its appearance, the digital is electronic nothingness ... its appearance from electronic lino is one with its analog transformation' (Massumi 2002, 138).

The analogue is what actualizes the digital according to this line of thought. The rise of digital technologies and their spillover effect in political and international affairs has essentially brought forth a somewhat artificial binary – rather than an uneven transition – between analogue and digital politics.

Analogue politics, diplomacy, war, and peace did not need to be labelled as such prior to the rise of digitality (Hassan 2021,384). It is only as part of a bifurcated analogy with the digital that we can make sense of the analogue qualities in IR and its implications for the limits of peacemaking.

Implications for War and Peace

State Dynamics, Diplomacy, and International Order

A first step in this study is to explain the analogy of analogue and digital forms of international relations, and its relevance for peace. When applied to IR, the concept of analogue describes the state of affairs in IR during the twentieth century whereby thinking and acting operate on the logic of hierarchy, inequality, and exclusion, bounded by territorial sovereignty and existing north–south and internal class hierarchies. Analogue forms of international relations and IR theory pertained to a territorially situated world of international relations involving huge distances, centralized governments, territorial sovereignty, the states-system, and the development of inter-governmental and non-governmental transnational institutions (Spykman 1994). This was a world in which time, space, and technology interacted with states and societies in a relatively predictable manner described by theories of political realism and liberalism, predicated upon a basic balance of power system and its related diplomatic processes. It was a world that could be scaled, recognized, and related to regardless of the prevalence of violence and injustice.

The state was seen as a Leviathan with Weberian characteristics, balanced externally by other 'Great Powers' and shaped, reformed, or resisted by social and revolutionary movements, thus forced into an internal social contract. International relations were marked by geopolitical power, which drove state-centric wars, institutional balancing, and social frameworks for engagement and critique which also engaged with civil conflict. Social, cultural, and environmental considerations were secondary to ideological, geopolitical, and geo-economic forces (Kennan 1947; Scholvin and Wigell 2018). Analogue wars were fought through violent and non-violent means with tools ranging from traditional espionage, coercive diplomacy, to battlefield manoeuvres and physical. In turn, peace spanned a victor's peace to negative peace as a result (Galtung 1969; Richmond 2005). In an analogue world, matters concerning war and peace had a human, space, and time dimension. Conflicts were fought on land and for land, material resources, and the control of populations and strategic sites. The sites where peace processes have taken place have been place-based spaces with status, such as national or regional capitals, or Vienna, Geneva, Paris, London, or New York, using conference venues, diplomatic offices, or sometimes military sites. And war and peace were temporal and sequential phenomena, representing a continuous struggle for power, domination, as well as for peace and stability.

The diplomacy and organizational tasks were complex and vast. This can be seen in the logistics required to coordinate and follow up on the Congress of Vienna in 1815, the scale of the Congress of Berlin in 1878, and the Paris Peace Treaty in 1919. One should also consider the risks of the Atlantic Charter meetings in 1941, the exponential increase in the scale of the annual UN General Assemblies since 1946, the meetings on UN Treaties and Conventions such as the Decolonisation Convention of 1960, and the International Covenant on Civil and Political Rights of 1966: the International Covenant on Economic, Social, and Cultural Rights also of 1966; Convention on the Elimination of All Forms of Discrimination against Women of 1979; as well as the GATT and World Trade Organizations meetings. They all attest not only to the scale and potential of international diplomacy and related institutional development in an analogue framework but also to their acute limitations.

Overall, the resultant global political architecture was formed by war, imperialism, ideological competition, and trade, leaving legacies of violence and inequality. These legacies also drove the creation of multilateral institutions and organizations, law (including recent attempts at developing the Law of Peace) (UN General Assembly 2016), as well as the expectation of expanded social networks and political frameworks of rights and emancipation, as liberal institutions and social movements expanded their operation within the state and the states-system. All of this was conducted through a physical infrastructure dependent upon complex diplomacy, logistics, the mediation of different political interests, legal and bureaucratic systems, often via enormous conferences and meetings over great distance.

Challenges to Order: Social Movements, Civil Society, and the Expansion of Rights

Analogue social frameworks for critique engendered a range of early advocacy networks (Keck and Sikkink 1998, 10), which advocated for social change and rights (abolition of slavery and disarmament being two) as well as of states and capital, but they worked within the context of the technologies of the day, which were more suited to territorial forms of sovereignty and centralized, state-centric political authority. Multilateralism and the development of civil society were tenuous in this framework given the logistical challenges. Peacemaking in the analogue world rested upon slow, face-to-face, elitist diplomacy, and institutions, operating in human time, amplified by twentieth-century technologies, in which the industrial West and elite classes dominated. Positionality within the hierarchy was closely guarded, along with the sources of state and political, economic power and the processes of institutional and social governmentality. This facilitated a mainstream debate based upon the eternal nature of state-units, hierarchies, and interests (and their state-based clashes) or alternatively, in idealist and liberal terms, the universal nature of human rights guaranteed by a mixture of state and international law.

The vast scale of logistics to implement and maintain such international tools and institutions also in part explains their difficulty in bringing them to fruition and later, their implementation. Yet, the international institutions and peace frameworks that emerged by the twentieth century eventually responded, to a limited degree at least, to their own limitations and the demands of social movements (such as with the 1950 Uniting for Peace Resolution of the General Assembly) (UN General Assembly 1950), especially in the areas of rights, injustice and inequality after the Universal Declaration of Human Rights (UDHR) with legal, political, and military instruments. They slowly tried to address obstacles to critical agency and expanding claims for rights (Arendt 1951; DeGooyer et al. 2018, 4; Moyn 2018, 153–72) through the development of new tools such as rights, development, peacekeeping, and peacebuilding, and increasingly through their connection with what became known as global civil society (Kaldor 2003). Yet, they operated within the context of inherited imperial power and geopolitical political frameworks, meaning any radicalism was tempered.

The analogue system of international relations thus protected long-standing hierarchies and was based upon geopolitics and territorial sovereignty as ways of organizing power and capital. Historical processes of state formation in the long term (Tilly 1990) legitimated a nationalist narrative about the origins and current status of state and international order, despite their many shortcomings (Habsbawm 1990; Gellner 2006). Sovereignty, multilateralism, intervention, and law worked within this analogue framework. By necessity, it eventually came to have a liberal overlay of normativity that domesticated the worst attributes of geopolitics by focusing on democracy, rights, and trade, later known as the liberal peace (Doyle 1983, 207). Nevertheless, analogue forms of multilateralism were slow and cumbersome, often unwieldy in the industrial era in comparison to geopolitical and geo-economic rationality, which led to constant cycles and escalations of systemic and regional wars from the nineteenth century onwards. The endeavour to build peace in this context eventually led to the emergence of liberal international institutions to moderate interests, law, regional organizations, and NGOs to mobilize and condition social and political agency. They allowed more positive versions of peace to emerge (Galtung 1969), which in turn facilitated peacebuilding, statebuilding, and development praxis in the later twentieth century (while maintaining Eurocentric hegemony). However, they also established themselves as conservative systems of intervention, producing negative, liberal, or neoliberal forms of peace as a historical response to the long-standing geopolitical dynamics of violence and system collapse, as archaeologists have long argued (Tainter 1988).

Implications for Peace

Consequently, it can be argued that peace was determined and constructed in analogue international relations by the most hegemonic but centralized states and regional powers, territorially conceived and bounded, yet pursuing a sophisticated and well-supported foreign policy designed to mitigate war. Their behaviour was moderated by global institutions and trade. Analogue approaches to peacemaking operated through face-to-face governance extended discursively through policy doctrines (this being the early point of many of the arguments of liberal theorists like Locke and Paine) (Locke 1988; Paine 2000). It had a historical presence, and a social order that responded to political authority, according to power, autonomy and self-determination, and rights and law, as Rousseau (1978) argued. Such states represented a 'home' but were connected through tenuous human, social, military, political, and economic relations with other states. The natural environment was not seen as an agent within such theorizing (Ostrom 1990), as politics assumed extractive political and economic models (Harvey 2005).

The individual and society were subservient to states in this framework and their agency was amplified by access to certain 'heavy' industrial technologies, heavily regulated by law and by capital which at the same time carries forward old imperial or racial hierarchies (though perhaps not explicitly) (Mazower 2012; Mishra 2012). A hierarchy of states remained in international relations, which represented 'peace' in a status quo form, mitigated by international organizations. This hierarchy has been relatively unchanged over the time that it has been measured in the Human Development Index. In other words, peace in the analogue international system maintained a natural, eternal, and unchanging framework involving acute lines of division and inequality. It was formed mainly in the eighteenth century, reshaped in the twentieth century under conditions of industrial-scale war making, decolonization, liberal internationalist, and capitalist responses, and is shifting again with the advent of new actors and new technologies (Simmons 2011; Fritsch 2014; Stuenkel 2015).

Peace in analogue IR thus operated within the parameters and material structures of the Westphalian state system. It was heavily territorialist and geopolitical, tending towards the authoritarian or hegemonic (Cox 1981), thus providing the structural constraints against which the state, humans and society struggle in extractive mode. This struggle has produced a series of normative critiques of power, evil, geopolitics, hierarchy, and capital (Hurrell 2008). These structures were eventually modified and mitigated post–World War II and post–Cold War by the liberal international system: namely human rights, democracy, and development, embodied in the capacities of the UN, but strictly limited by the power of dominant states (such as key Security Council members). This whole system is determined by the scale, hierarchy, and time frames denoted by territoriality (Elden 2011).

When Fukuyama offered his twentieth-century revision of Kant's Perpetual Peace to general acclaim, 'The End of History and the Last Man' effectively marked the apogee of analogue international relations. Its logic operated within the constraints of industrialized states and their economic and military power (with the additional caveat of the limits of capitalism and its impact on the natural environment) (Fukuyama 1988). Thus, analogue international relations were marked by several phases of conflict and responses in mainstream think-ing: the geopolitical phase, responded to by imperial and state balancing; the liberal international phase, responded to by strengthening multilateralism, glo-bal governance and international law; the post-colonial phase, to which the response was self-determination, the limited expansion of rights, and the devel-opmental state; and the neoliberal and geo-economic phase, to which the post–Cold War response was limited forms of statebuilding and globalization (Barbara 2008, 307–8). The UN system, international law, human rights, and democracy (Doyle 1983), resting on Cold War policies of 'containment' (Kennan 1984) and augmented by the Helsinki Convention, and the Washington Consensus were perhaps the most well-known elements of the analogue order connected with peace (Pugh 2005).

Conclusion

After World War II, peace emerged from a liberal overlay of normativity that domesticated the worst attributes of geopolitics and geo-economics by focusing on democracy, human rights, and trade, followed quickly by the emergence of development and humanitarian strategies, associated with a further develop-ment of the liberal peace (Doyle 1983; Rist 2003). However, analogue, face-to-face, capital-centric (and normally in the Global North) forms of multilateralism were slow and cumbersome, ultimately unwieldy. Diplomacy, mediation, and later peacekeeping, development and humanitarianism ironed out the flaws of the geopolitical and post-colonial international system, during the Cold War and after, to the degree that it was able to maintain a ragged legitimacy during the latter half of the twentieth century, but such tools were not able to support the advanced and expanded rights claims that have emerged with decolonization and since the collapse of the USSR.

Geopolitical and geo-economic rationality prospered in an analogue system of international relations, driving peacekeeping, mediation, and later, peacebuilding, statebuilding, and development, towards becoming conservative systems of intervention. They produced negative, liberal, or neoliberal forms of peace as can be seen in the cases spanning Cambodia to Bosnia, Kosovo, and Timor Leste in the 1990s (Richmond and Jason Franks 2008; Visoka 2017). This system's legitimacy was further undermined by the legacy of the War on Terror and the Afghanistan and Iraq statebuilding engagements of the 2000s. Its culmination led to an 'interventionary order' (Richmond 2020), in which intervention was designed to protect state security and capital accumulation, along with the more secondary features of democracy and human rights via an enabling state, supported by donors, regional actors such as the European Union (EU), International Financial Institutions (IFIs), and the UN system. Authoritarian forms of peacebuilding outcomes have been its eventual result (Lewis, and John and Megoran 2018). This evolution, which saw the liberal and rights-oriented nature of peacemaking expand as a discursive framework in to liberal peacebuilding by the 1990s, has been marked by a huge gap between the growing aims associated with peace and the emergence of blockages in peace processes, stalemates, reversions to war or to previous political orders (Haggard and Robert Kaufman 2021, 1–4), frozen conflicts (Smetana and Ludvik 2019), authoritarian outcomes, and the rise of revisionist actors on the international stage (Ratelle and Souleimanov 2016; Zheng and Hang 2020; Doshi 2021, 66; Strasheim and Subindra Bogati 2021, 354; Hellmüller 2022;). At the same time, the development of new tools, possibilities, and strategies for peacemaking has been acknowledged in the international system in the UN system and amongst its repertoire of tools, by states, donors, and global civil society (UN Department of Peace Operations 2021). It is hard to say that their arrival has improved peacemaking or peacebuilding, increased its efficiency or effectiveness, or addressed local political claims within a peace process – beyond rhetoric and aspiration. Digital international relations are still driven by reinvented power relations amongst shifting actors motivated by similar issues of territorial sovereignty, extraction, regional influence, and domestic order. Many of the strategies that have emerged connected to peace are microtools that facilitate the workings of analogue processes and tools or amass data that cannot yet be analysed clearly.

Interventionary processes designed to create peace remain preoccupied with the state model they apply and processes they use, as well as their adoption of both by local populations: effectively reiterating the post–Cold War interest in norm transfer, local ownership, and the 'local turn'. This is still effectively appended to post-imperial and post-Soviet models of liberal peace, neoliberal statehood, and development, despite the advent of digital shifts in IR. The shift from a quasi-trusteeship approach to local ownership has created problems for peacebuilding's normative legitimacy when understood as an amalgamation of subaltern claims (either at the state or social level) about global justice, which look unlikely to be solved by digital peace solutions as they are so far constituted. The contradictions of peacebuilding now seem too powerful for its legitimacy to survive at both the international and the local scales without major modification given the transition from analogue to digital forms of order, however. Liberal peacebuilding and statebuilding structures focused mainly on the viability of the post-conflict state and the interests of major powers (global and regional) at the expense of the everyday needs of the individuals and communities they claim to assist, ignoring for the most part transnational networks and relations that both fed conflicts and supported peacemaking at the societal level.

For example, Bosnian politics are still divided and deadlocked twenty years after the Dayton Agreements; the Cyprus peace process is in a continuous stalemate; the Northern Ireland peace process is only superficially a 'success-story'; security and development are provided in Cambodia mainly through authoritarianism and an extractive or subsistence economy; finally, in many other cases, similar local complaints are voiced about the absence of a peace dividend, of the state's public goods, and the (social and political) distance of international organizations, despite their presence in those countries (Richmond 2014, 9). Similarly, although studies have shown that peacekeeping is fairly effective in reducing the likelihood of war's recurrence (Fortna 2008; Goldstein 2011), this often represents an admission that only the worst can be dealt with under the rudimentary, analogue terms that international order provided during this era.

The question for our next section is, therefore, what can new digital capacities, tools, and frameworks do to address the shortcomings if liberal peacebuilding, neoliberal peace, hybrid political orders, and the loss of legitimacy of the UN's peacemaking framework? Can they help facilitate security, rights, democracy, reconciliation, justice, and sustainablity, as the direction of travel of scholarship on peace and conflict studies suggests would be necessary?[5]

---

[5] For an overview of the direction such scholarship has taken, see Richmond et al. 2016.

3 Peace in Digital International Relations

Introduction

As has been widely acknowledged, digital technologies have emerged as one of the most significant new frontiers of an increasingly dynamic field of world politics, spurring developments in the nature of war, violence, governance, and peacemaking. In essence, digital technologies are characterized by their capacity to aggregate and compute data, as well as direct, index, and manipulate social reality (Peters 2016, 103). The concept of the digital and digitality describes the technological and informational domain characterized by discontinuity and the disruption of forms, scales, and affairs. As Hassan maintains, 'digitality is the logic of discontinuity inserted as mediating form into wherever it can reach – which is almost everywhere' (Hassan 2021, 386).

Discontinuity means the transferal of humans from one domain of social and political life to another. This new nexus claimed not to be material, relational, and processual – but rather one which is networked, discrete, alienating, hard to anticipate, and out of social sight and control (Hassan 2016, 91). It is most often used and controlled by existing political and economic elites, who are imbricated in power relations and systems that predate peacemaking tools, however, and applied for military and political uses, as well as for profit and governance. This section examines the implications of this critical perspective for peace in IR.

Critical Perspectives of Digital Peace in IR

How does the digital shape peace in international relations? State, international institutions, and civil society tend to innovate, adjust to, and accept new technologies as part of a struggle for interests, norms, and rights (Milner, and Solstad 2021). This might be because of competition and a fear of vulnerability, as well as pressure from other rivals, including transnational and non-state actors, or because of an attempt to embed norms of pluralism and cooperation. Though the potential of the digital shift is perhaps as great as the industrial shift earlier, it carries all the attendant risks of war, as experienced after the 'long peace' between the Congress of Vienna (of dubious provenance) and the breakdown of domestic and international order from the beginning of the twentieth century, when industrialized, imperial power escaped the peace systems that had constrained nineteenth century states and power relations (Kennedy 1987). The 'long peace' was replaced by another, rough, long peace (marred by northern hegemony, wars in the global south as well as the structural conflict of the Cold War) under US hegemony from 1945 (Gaddis 1986; Pinker 2011), and this analogue, bipolar, and then unipolar but multilateral order is now in the process of breaking down.

Unlike the last breakdown from around 1914–45, the question is how might we prevent war as we shift into the digital era after neo/liberal hegemony? (Keohane and Nye 1977).

Critical debates have long pointed to the contradictory and cumbersome nature of mainstream IR in analogue mode (George 1994). Post-structuralism pointed to identity, fluidity, mobility, difference, and critical agency over cumbersome systems of sovereignty (Walker 1993); critical theory pointed to the limits of territorialism and the need for global systems of legitimate authority, and justice (Held 2004; Weber 2004) constructivism pointed to the social construction of political frameworks, institutions, the state, and the international; post-colonialism pointed to political and social hybridity and a more radical process of decolonization; gender debates and environmental discussions opened up new dimensions of inequality in a range of ways, from the ontological to the methodological (Sylvester 2002; Connolly 2017). Critical work on security and post-colonialism has also pointed in this direction, raising questions about new forms of emancipation particularly those driven by subaltern perspectives on peace (Williams 2005, 135).

The 'digital' is a term that appears to capture the contemporary zeitgeist, yet it clearly has a bifurcated character. It may on the one hand signify leaderless, dextrous, and decentralized networks, nodes, and associations between varied political, social, and economic groups, both human and technological. It depends on new technology aimed at disrupting existing political modes of organization and entrenched power relations within analogue IR and appears to be the definitional foundation (and at the same time end-objective) of civil society organizations active in conflict regions, peace technologists, and peace activists. However, on the other hand, it may also extend existing and historical centres of legitimate authority or power relations – governmentalities – that are ambivalent about rights and everyday political claims (Coward 2017, 443–4). For instance, the concept of digital war has been employed to describe '[t]he ways in which digital technologies and media are transforming how wars are fought, experienced, lived, represented, reported, known, conceptualised, remembered and forgotten'.[6] A concept of digital peace is required as a response.

Significant Changes in Paradigm?

Digital rationalities are ontologically different in scale because the key dimensions of the analogue – space/distance, time, centralized power/boundaries/ knowledge – depend on territory, sovereignty, industrialization, and capital. Digital capacities mean these dynamics are now fundamentally changed

---

[6] The *Journal of Digital War*: www.digital-war.org/digital-war-introduction.

(Knox and Walford 2016). They are either extended in reach and speed or more fundamentally altered with new dimensions or attributes. Whereas analogue systems and frameworks of thinking and acting on the world depend on the continuity of relations between actants in a fixed architecture, in the digital world relations operate on the logic of disruption and diffraction, with either the reinforcement of older regimes and their extension or the emergence of new regimes as a consequence.

Although, as noted in the Introduction, the digital environment consists of a great variety of tools with an equally diverse number of users, developers and their interests, a common denominator for digital technologies and how they change the dynamics *for* peace can also be drawn out. Space, distance, and time have been altered by new technologies, and transactions take place at much greater distances and speeds (as with information, capital, or missiles) (Owen 2015). Law, rights, and political institutions still operate in analogue scales, however. Network theory and work on global assemblages have made this clear, but the extent to which this undermines socio-political ethics essential for peace is only now becoming clearer (Coward 2017). Digital technologies may thus tend to constitute new forms of politics with far-reaching implications for peace, replacing and disrupting older parts of the international architecture, even though they remain necessary. New digital frontiers such as big data, algorithms, machine learning, as well as virtual reality represent new features that are reshaping social, economic, and political relations within and between states (Richterich 2018). As a result of digital politics, the old rational-actor model is being taken to an extreme, apparently removing the social and the political from the equations of IR. Knowledge may now be democratized in digital form, but power has shifted from its control of territory to the control of networks and access to them as a means of control and governance. Power may thus be partly re-centralized (via a populist association between regimes, practices, and capital) rather than democratized (the demos are dispersed and fractured) under the emerging conditions of digital governmentality (Owen 2015, 30).

Thus, IR, peace, security, and order, are no longer centred on the territorial state (if they ever full were), but on an amorphous, complex, and unstable set of networks and their nodes, with fluid goals, all dependent upon the next technological enhancement, which shifts IR's potential and capacities again. Knowledge is no longer universal as in liberalism and science but must be disruptive of established consensus and patterns, and is driven by technology, *meaning that any resulting peace framework would have to attempt to stabilize systems designed to be unstable and contradictory* (contradicting the liberal peace framework that prospered when states and institutions were stable in a universal rights framework) (see Owen 2015, 38).

Digital frameworks fundamentally aim to undermine the checks and balances that maintained existing power relations at social, state, and international levels of analysis, partly by bypassing them with new technologies and frameworks, partly through disruption, and partly through collapsing analogue, material conceptions of time, space, distance, and power. Scale jumping ensues, unsettling old political hierarchies, which nevertheless will respond. Digital frameworks thus refine and invigorate hegemonic, interest-driven practices of intervention for peace, security, and order, making them fast, invisible, and connected to economic interests, as opposed to the public and rights or security-oriented peace process of the analogue era. Perhaps designed to support hegemony in international order, it is likely that this would lead to multipolarity and inter-regional tensions, with little in the way of related peacemaking capacities from within the new digital layers of IR. Such risks outweigh to a large extent their benefits for civil society and transnational or transversal mobilization for rights, justice, and security. They also help explain the growing authoritarianism that arises after peace processes or during peacebuilding during this digital era (von Billerbeck and Tansey 2019).

Networks versus Sovereignty

Networks have always been the historical backbone of social order, often hidden and extremely resilient; they have been a significant feature of archaeological and anthropological data and theory on the collapse or survival of societies of minor and major scale throughout history (Tainter 1988). Early on after the Cold War they became essential for civil society, and global civil societies rights and democratization advocacy (Finnemore and Sikkink 1998). Later they became significant for transversal processes of peace formation as hybrid forms of peace emerged in places as distant as Timor Leste or Kosovo (Richmond and Franks 2008; Visoka 2012; Richmond 2016; Richmond and Pogodda 2016; Visoka 2016; Visoka and Richmond 2017). Nevertheless, their digitization allows for a fundamental amplification of their significance (Castells 2009, 21).

This happens in two ways, one of which is the increased connectivity between different groups, mainly through the use of social media. The Israeli-Iranian or Greco-Turkish friendship networks on Facebook, for example, consist of people whose persuasion (that peace and any rapprochement towards it are more desirable than conflict) would not have been known nor made evident without the opportunity offered by new technology. Instead, any such networks would have been limited to people who already knew of (and had access to) like-minded people from 'the other side' in face-to-face mode. The second way in which the significance of networks is amplified is a direct result of the above, namely the amount of information being produced, circulated, and accessed by an ever-increasing number of network participants. This aids not only their visibility but also their participation within these networks. This is true about citizen journalism, or the ability that any mobile phone owner has to record instances of injustice, discrimination, and/or brutality in real time: their intervention reaches bigger audiences, thus having the capacity to influence political outcomes to an extent that would not have been possible in an analogue world (of course, it has also become clear that such potential can easily be inverted).

Significantly, digital time is not linear nor constrained by material factors: progress or backsliding – features of liberal thought – are too simplistic to understand the dimensions, fluctuations and incredible speeds, and potentially intergenerational nature of digital time. It may well be argued here that, on the one hand, all of this has augmented humanity, changed society, altered the nature of the state (and its relevance), influenced global governance, and created new forms of global collaboration. On the other hand, however, there is an undisputed rush by states (as hegemonic actors par excellence) to control as much of the digital time and the flow of information in it, thus fomenting political, social, and economic inequalities, injustice and, in some cases, conflict. As such, implications arise for war and peace, for law and institutions, for their intersections with the environment, markets and capital, and further technological advances.

In particular, since such digital technologies are employed by both democratic and authoritarian states and by parties in internal conflicts, the function of digital platforms operates through the logic of contradiction (or double-movements in Polanyi's (1944) felicitous phrase) and can significantly challenge, or reinforce, traditional ways of thinking, doing, and acting in the world. As articulated by Peace Direct (2020, 21), a peacebuilding organization:

> In many ways, digital technologies are a double-edged sword. They can empower people to create meaningful opportunities for change, they can enable marginalised groups to participate in activities equally, and can be used by citizens to hold governments and power holders to account. However, these same technologies can strengthen the ability of those perpetuating conflict to engage in sophisticated censorship and surveillance, and disrupt and divide communities with dangerous consequences. Indeed, digital technologies are increasingly a powerful force that is fundamentally altering both peace and conflict dynamics.

The digital shift represents a major change for the international system from being based upon Euro-centric notions of territorial sovereignty to the development and control of networks relating to key states, capital, technology, knowledge/information, as well as more traditional class, diplomatic, and military networks.

Coward has described its elevation of networks as a 'pathological sovereignty' by way of a replacement for rights, identity, and territoriality, which seem more likely to merely extend the pathologies of earlier forms of sovereignty. This operates through fantasies of the precise application of force, governance through 'nudges' (Thaler and Cass 2008), and the ability to bypass ethics and culture (Coward 2017, 444 and 452–56). It is part of a century-long development at least, relating to an increasingly precise political praxis for social and international intervention, select-ive de-territorialization, and the increasing speed of transactions, partially moder-ated by global governance. Communications and transport advances have changed the structural impediments of nature and geography, shifting the speeds and distance through and over which civil society, the state, and international actors can operate significantly (as Virilio also pointed out in the context of the Gulf War for the military) (Virilio 2002). Yet, access to knowledge, and its production, has significantly improved and widened. Positionalities across time and space have become much more discernible, even for the subalterns of IR/international relations (Shilliam 2010).

This has enormous implications for rights and justice claims on local and global scales, whether related to violence or inequality, war, gender, or the natural environment (Sylvester 2011; Mac Ginty and Richmond 2013). Digital technologies amplify the power of people and networks, as well as the state, capital and the 'international', but not in the same ways or at the same levels. Significant inequalities remain and are amplified, and contradictions are becom-ing even more politicized. A digital struggle is forming between individuals and society, the state, and the international and techno-capital, with shifting net-works and alliances forming, to push forward rights claims or to reject them. They contest the nature of the state, the extent of the political community (local to global), the priorities of politics and IR particularly relating to access to new rights (Owen 2015, 35; Slaughter 2004, 283). In this struggle analogue concepts like territory, borders and institutions are little more than obstacles to digital political agendas: whether expanded rights or expanded geo-economic power. However, the contradictions and conflicts caused by the ragged concept of territorial sovereignty, the race for centralized power within the state, regional geopolitics, and limited international political will to intervene, protect rights, and make peace, remain substantial.

Global Civil Society

Yet, the new digital tools, dynamics, and capacities have been useful for 'global civil society' and its 'norm cascades' in the last few decades (Finnemore and Sikkink 1998; Kaldor 2003), as well as for populist nationalism, and the disruption of political organizations (such as Russian campaigns aimed at NATO, the EU, Ukraine and other states in the region, as well as possible interventions through social media and right-wing capital in the US election in 2017 and the Brexit referendum in the UK in 2016) (Barber 2016, *The Economist* 2016). While the early literature indicated that cascades of liberal civil society activism would take over the state and reshape the international system, authoritarian power, and the markets, offering expanded rights, more mature viewpoints to how long-entrenched power relations are now reinforcing themselves through digital strategies which enable power to shift into atmospheric modes, transcending the state, sovereignty, and 'legacy' international architecture of the twentieth century (Owen 2015, 172–81; et al. 2021).

While digital international relations are heavily networked, this means that control of networks and their nodes is vital for hegemony, and though digital IR might seem to promise to devolve power because networks are relational, they are also utilitarian, transactional, and may well reflect established power relations too (relating, say, to the military–industrial complex, or elite, state, and global capital. Networks also maintain hierarchies, meaning that interests may now proliferate even faster across these widening networks. Thus, this may offer a form of digital governmentality, designed to limit, block, and counter the expansion of social movements, civil society, justice and global rights frameworks and their related connection of peace, security, and development with emancipatory claims. As Farrell and Newman showed, states that control the hubs where most of the information flows to and from can 'weaponize networks to gather information or choke off economic and information flows, discover and exploit vulnerabilities, compel policy change, and deter unwanted actions' (Farrell and Newman 2019, 45). Private enterprises, too, appear to aid state efforts for total surveillance and control: at the 2022 World Economic Forum, the President of Alibaba Group presented his company's efforts to develop an individual carbon footprint tracker that traced each customer's purchases, dietary preferences, travel plans, and more (Lawton 2022). At the same forum, the CEO of Pfizer explained his company's efforts for the development of a pill with a tiny chip that would alert relevant authorities that the pill had been ingested (Loffredo 2022). It is hard to imagine how states and elites would not want to capitalize on such technologies to quell or to deter dissent (as was arguably the case with the freezing of bank accounts of Canadian truck drivers' protesting Covid vaccination mandates) (Loh 2022).

If anything, however, this argument and the examples provided in the following section highlight the fact that digital technology has enabled and/ or empowered civil society to challenge analogue structures and modi operandi in ways that were not fathomable before the turn of the century – and to do so with incomparable speed: Civil society is composed of those more or less spontaneously emergent associations, organizations, and movements that, attuned to how societal problems resonate in the private life spheres, distil and transmit such reactions in amplified form to the public sphere (Habermas 1989, 27).

Digital technologies have allowed civil society to become global and more political, consisting of diverse, decentralized (sometimes leaderless) net-works and organizations that connect and expand horizontally, prioritizing communication and deliberation that leads to coordinated action (Juris 2005), often in the form of 'dotcauses' (Clark and Themudo 2006). Historically speaking, most of the advances in peacemaking and the inter-national peace architecture have come from evolving networks of social and scholarly participants, with the occasional elite actor and policymaker included. Now these linkages are more plausible and more active than ever before. Whereas civil society was traditionally considered to be 'a substitute for the state', the qualitative characteristics ascribed to global civil society by the use of digital technologies have led states and authorities to the realization that the current form of civil society can also be 'a pressure on the state' (Kaldor and Kostovicova 2021, 330). This would explain authori-tarian states' – from Russia, China, Cambodia, to Myanmar, and Syria – subsequent rush to control information and networks alike, and maintain hierarchies and domination, and to turn civil society into an extension of the state, or of global and regional hegemons.

Digital Peace or Digital Governmentality?

At the policy level, digital peace is still often conceived of through analogue logics of reasoning (Betz and Stevens 2013, 147–64), or digital insertions are merely viewed as facilitating old approaches. In recent years a central feature of securing peace in the digital age has been the efforts to enhance the normative and operational aspects of cybersecurity, namely the conditions for 'an open, secure, peaceful and accessible cyberspace' (UN 2013, 2). In international law, the concept of cyber peace has been deployed to describe normative and legal frameworks which seek to regulate the conduct of cyber activities among state and non-state actors in international relations. Although the subject matter concerning cybersecurity is slightly different from the traditional security challenges, the logic, and approaches for addressing existing and potential cyber threats and thus promoting digital peace have been similar to those applied previously in the analogue IR. This implies that the reductionist goal of regulating digital peace is to 'maximize peaceful benefits' and 'curtail unintended consequences and malicious use' (UN General Assembly 2020, para. 47). In other words, cyber peace is more akin to analogue peace translated for the digital age. It has a preventive and reactive logic to the perceived structural and situational factors deemed as threats to digital peace.

For instance, mirroring Galtung's concept of positive peace, Shackelford (2014, 357) argues that [c]yber peace is more than simply the inverse of cyber war; what might a more nuanced view of cyber peace resemble? First, stakeholders must recognize that a positive cyber peace requires not only addressing the causes and conduct of cyber war, but also cybercrime, terrorism, espionage, and the increasing number of incidents that overlap these categories.

It also involves the effort of major powers to engage in dialogue to regulate Internet governance and the application of digital and cyber technologies beyond state borders. It therefore aims to mirror treaty-making efforts in the analogue age, possible to extend their capacity but not their emancipatory content. The starting point of this analogue approach to digital peace has been an extension of the key principles governing the existing international political and legal order. The main aspect is the position taken by the UN and a majority of states that international law and the UN Charter are applicable to cyber threats and cyberwar.

Deriving from this UN-centred but rather conservative understanding of digital peace as a mitigation and extension of state authority and liberal international order, state sovereignty and international norms continue to apply to the conduct of ICT-related activities within the analogue understanding of state authority, responsibility and territoriality – as evidenced by a 2021 report by the UN Human Rights Council Advisory Committee, where the onus for 'best practices' falls onto states (UN Human Rights Council 2021, 10–11). Moreover, rights-based frameworks and inter-state cooperation against cyber threats are seen as crucial to building confidence and capacities for sustaining digital peace, representing something of a contradictory epistemological and policy framing. For instance, the UN Secretary-General's report on the state of global peace in 2020, reiterated that, [t]here is a need for new legal and ethical standards on the use of such technologies to foster trust, peace, and stability. They must be grounded in internationally agreed instruments, which provide the framework for the protection of, and respect for, human rights, peace and security. (UN General Assembly 2020, para. 47).

Mainstream digital international relations thus extend realism and liberalism into digital governmentality connected to surveillance capital (Zuboff 2019b, 9), designed for corporate profit, and scientific innovation connected with stabilizing state, western, and economic power. More importantly such a rationality is design to manage or quell the political claims of the world's populations for global justice, reflecting 'peacekeeping as riot control' to preserve a hegemonic order in Pugh's (2005) felicitous framing. Yet, this damages attempts to reconstruct legitimate political authority after war, as can be seen with the reversion to authoritarian power in Cambodia (Morgenbesser 2019), or the regression of the peace process in Colombia (Hristov 2006). Digital international relations and diplomatic interactions tend to be virtual rather than face to face, perhaps even more based upon interests because they lack the potential for empathy or interest in justice, society and culture than its analogue version was (Foucault 1982; Latour 2005; Badouard et al. 2016). Its virtual, networked, accelerated mode is merely a precursor to the next stages in the development of war, power, diplomacy, and trade (Virilio 2002; Der Derian 2013). These next stages build on data, access, and networks to bypass the established mitigating systems of international relations, including the shift to future remote operations (utilizing drones for warfare, peacekeeping or intelligence, connected to power and hegemony, etc.), and the automation of international relations more extensively.

Under the emerging digital framework, power may shift from access and control of the key institutions of the territorial state and economy as under the analogue mode (for example security services, the military, political institutions, infrastructure, the UN, IFIs, donor system, etc.). It may shift to the control of networks between them, nodes around the network, their modes of operation, their speed and access, as well as the capacity to harvest and process related data in digital international relations (Castells 2009, 44 and 419).

The emergence of an enhanced capacity to network through technology speeds up the application of power and interests through process data and related decision-making, the coordination of policy goals, and the ability to extend governmentality. So far this has been very cumbersome in the analogue system of UN peacekeeping, mediation, peacebuilding, and development, for example. This is the basis of Latour's conception of the actor-network (Latour 2005). It appears to promise more efficient and effective connections between technology, data, the state and international, as well as with research, capital, the military, and industry (but omits to engage with the problem of the limits of the natural world itself) (Chandler 2018, 21). Simultaneously, it facilitates activities and networks of advocacy and resistance pertaining to rights, equality, and justice. Time and distance collapse under its conditions, as has long been argued (Graham 1998), provoking heavily modified social claims for justice (Owen 2015), in the changing context of the Anthropocene (Crutzen 2002; Dürbeck, et al. 2016).

These developments may well facilitate mobility, communication, expanded rights and social mobilization: including equality under decentralized power-systems and democratized forms of knowledge; new and more relevant forms of legitimate political authority, perhaps through peace formation (Richmond 2016); as well as a greater understanding of the cultural, aesthetic/visual, and normative dimensions of difference and cooperation.[7] Critical thinking about the Anthropocene and the risks of human impact on the ecosystem provides early hints about the tensions between it, and the limits of digital international relations.

However, digital international relations are also dominated by power, along with networks connecting new actors, with new interests. This connects with analogue sites of power such as classes, the state, military capacity, and capital. It represents a form of digital governmentality that displaces its former liberal and neo-liberal versions, very much akin to 'surveillance capitalism' (Aradau and Blanke 2017; Zuboff 2019a). Zuboff (2019b, 9) argues that the latter, . . . runs contrary to the early digital dream . . . it strips away the illusion that the networked form has some kind of indigenous moral content, that being 'connected' is somehow intrinsically pro-social, innately inclusive, or naturally tending towards the democratisation of knowledge . . . At its core surveillance capitalism is parasitic and self-referential.

Thus, digital international relations create a context for rethinking the concept of peace that is partly characterized by a tendency towards disruption after the failure of various types of liberal governance in the analogue mode (Chandler 2018, 159). But disruption is an unpredictable dynamic, and it also risks undermining the entire system. Whether it offers progress for global civil society, rights, democracy, and sustainability, or is regressive and enforces neoliberal power or geopolitical inequality, is open for debate. More critical versions of digital IR raise even deeper questions of sustainability, equality, and representation (perhaps following the logic of critical debates about the Anthropocene), expanding the mobilization of social actors across its networks, utilizing its flexibility and speed, but always in opposition to digital governmentality to engage with long term questions of sustainability.

As stabilization increasingly appears to be the main interest of western hegemonic order, revision of the international order is the main interests of

---

[7] The UN's Global Pulse project is one example of a response, through which UN agencies and private organizations offer the capacity through 'big data' and global social networks to engage in humanitarianism. See www.unglobalpulse.org ; Duffield 2019,153.

the BRICs, and rights and development the main interest of much weaker social movements and civil society, it is unlikely that digital peace will support the latter, make peace plausible in a multipolar order, or facilitate western hegemony. This suggests the contours of a large-scale clash rather than a mediation of social or international differences.

The Expansion of Rights and Justice

Conversely, since the 1990s the pace and scale of the expansion of rights frameworks and inclusion (particularly of social and civil actors) have increased very substantially and in part this has capitalized on the potential of new technologies, networks, speed, distance jumping, and more substantial access to verifiable knowledge. For example, the number of NGOs registered globally with ECOSOC have increased from some 40 in 1948 to 3,382 in 2010.[8] There are an estimated 10 million NGOs now in existence around the world, many of them globally networked around liberal democratic, human rights, justice, humanitarian, development, and equality issues, connected to key international institutions and donors.[9]

This aspect of digital international relations promises an international emancipatory project, by connecting peace, development, and the international system to newer thinking about global justice (defined as historical, distributive, gender, and environmental) (Kohn 2013). This has been supported by the possibilities raised by digital 'global listening projects', a broad, interdisciplinary, and practical engagement, and their interpretation of subaltern claims for international reform. The UN's recent Sustaining Peace agenda (2016) is an example of this process, which has created enormous demands for progress from the state and the international architecture without giving either more resources.[10] Similarly, the Millennium Development Goals (MDG) (2000) and the Sustainable Development Goals (SDG) (2015) were based on a broadening and deepening epistemological framework, made possible by new technologies.[11] Under analogue conditions, previous consultations on peace or rights at the international level had tended to be limited to narrow constituted and extremely slow elite and diplomatic, institutional meetings, as with the promulgation of Wilson's Fourteen Points at the end of World War I or the development of the UDHR leading up to its announcement (see Grose

---

[8] Changes in the number of NGOs with consultative status with ECOSOC 1948 to 2010, www.statista.com/statistics/268357/changes-in-the-number-of-ngos-worldwide-since-1948/.

[9] See for example, 'The Top 100 NGOs 2013', The Global Journal. www.theglobaljournal.net/group/15-top-100-ngos-2013/article/585/.

[10] Advisory Group of Experts, 'The Challenge of Sustaining Peace' (UN, June 2015), 1–12.

[11] UN, *The Millennium Development Goals Report 2012* (New York: United Nations, 2012).

1996).[12] While such improvements have become clear, there is also significant opposition to digital global civil society, as can be seen in the growing marginalization (even by core actors such as the United States and the United Kingdom) of the role of International Governmental Organizations (IGO), of human rights agendas and cosmopolitan thought, and through defunding the NGO sector (Amnesty International 2019).

Conclusion

Clearly, digital international relations are much more complex than analogue international relations and potentially more unstable. Firstly, digital IR appears to represent a challenge to existing power relations that support inequality and injustice (an enhanced critical agency and 'ungovernmentality') (Pogodda and Richmond 2015), but it also enhances some of the existing order (particularly, the alliance between the state, military, capital, and technology). Secondly, it may be leaderless and uncoordinated, with complex, global networks as a constituency rather than a territorially bounded or identity-defined group of people framed by state sovereignty. Thus, it may also signal a shift of the location of power, from the state to social movements, or more likely towards centres of capital and technology. Initially, its uncoordinated and decentralized nature was significant for rights-based movements but later on more established forms of governmentality have moved into digital spaces. This partly helps explain the rise of authoritarianism once again in international relations, and during peace and reform processes, the challenge to democracy and rights, as well as to scholarship of emancipatory peace and its understanding of 'norm cascades' and expanding rights (Lewis et al. 2018). Thirdly, as an extension of the previous point, digital international relations projects power, shapes systems and practices, whether for hegemony or progress (Owen 2015), and thus points to two paths for rethinking peace.

One path may be a reflection of the enhanced rights claims made by conflict-affected populations more able to build a political agenda in the context of the transversality, networks, speed, and mobility that digital international relations enable. This path points to the connection of peace with global justice. The other path rests on geopolitics and neoliberalism under digital governmentality and maintains a much more conservative international system.

Either way, the above argument suggests that international relations are undergoing significant change due to these wide and deep digital developments.

---

[12] See for example, Colonel House's discussions of the planning behind institution of the liberal peace framework, or post–World War II discussions on the United Nations High Commissioner for Refugees (UNHCR). See also: Grose 1996 and Morsink 1999.

The next section looks at the emancipatory potential of the new digital contributions to peace and evaluates them according to the sheer scale of change in international relations. Are they adequate, given we are effectively entering a new international era, or are they relatively minor additions. This may be especially the case when compared to the ability of digital international relations to be harnessed by conservative power structures with potentially revisionist goals: this means regional powers seeking to restore influence, global actors that seek to displace liberal hegemony (whether BRICS or regional powers), and political elites in conflict-affected societies which seek to find ways of preventing peace and reform from undermining their authority, legitimacy, and control. Effectively, such actors aim to influence, co-opt or completely reject the liberal international architecture. This means there may be a substantial gap between the digital augmentation of power in IR and the capacity of new digital peacemaking tools to respond to the conflicts and violence this gap creates. The next two sections will assess this claim in more detail.

4 The Promise of Digital Peacebuilding

Introduction

As we have argued, the liberal peacebuilding/neoliberal statebuilding model of the last quarter of a century lost social legitimacy within conflict-affected societies, to greater or lesser degrees, partly in parallel with the apparent decline of the status, political will, and reach of the United States (US), European Union (EU), and the United Kingdom (UK). Such approaches have lost traction with recipient political leaders (whom it often challenges) and who can choose from the 'new' (and not so selective) donors, including China (Tardy 2012). The liberal peace/neoliberal state model rapidly lost its post–Cold War appeal even though many civil society actors still may aspire to human security, human rights, democracy, and general prosperity. Furthermore, overcoming major political, social and economic inequality across local and international scales was partly ignored by peacebuilding, statebuilding, and development praxis for much of the last three decades, as they offered mainly small-scale and piecemeal approaches to what constituted major political claims of conflict-affected citizens. This is not to say that there is not wide local to global scale concern with what the new requirements for a positive peace, state, and international system may be. A new 'race' is on to define its peace architecture (UN General Assembly 2013) and its progressive elements are mainly being preserved and carried forward via the 'legacy' institutions related to the UN Secretariat, agencies, and global civil society, as well as some remaining donors.

Yet, their approaches remained grounded in analogue epistemological frameworks, and where digital methods, tools, and capacities have emerged their impact is often limited or controversial. This section outlines the implications of this tension for more positive applications of digital peace in the contemporary environment.

How Significant Are New Digital Tools?

The lack of access to peacebuilding, development, and humanitarian communities quickly became a major issue for the late twentieth-century peace system as it spilled over into the new century. Its 'bunkerised' compounds and secure and somewhat sanitized transport linkages indicated the pressure the liberal peacebuilding and neoliberal statebuilding system of the post–Cold War era were under, especially with the start of the War on Terror after 9/11 (see Duffield 2010). It has not been able to support conflict resolution or peace formation as strongly as was expected soon after 1990 (see Lederach 1995, 1997), and indeed by the 2010s, with conflicts and wars in Syria, Yemen, and Ukraine, the peacebuilding architecture and systems looked increasingly incapacitated. One would have expected policy actors to try to build higher levels of consent, consensus, and political will, as well as to connect more closely with local or networked systems of legitimate authority as a result. Some related efforts have been made, drawing on concepts ranging from human security, capacity building to local ownership (Tadjbakhsh and Chenoy 2006; UN Human Security Unit 2016). Despite the more recent signals offered by the Sustainable Development Goals of 2015 and the 'Sustaining Peace' agenda (UN General Assembly 2016; UN Security Council 2016; UN 2018), there has now arisen what appears to be a retrogressive dynamic, since the outbreak of the long Syrian war and the recent shift towards multipolarity in the international system that the Russian invasion of Ukraine and Chinese harrying of Taiwan indicate (see de Oliveira 2011; Kobrin 2020; Öniş and Kutlay 2020; Constantini and Santini 2022; Subedi 2022): the advancement of rights has been turned back across the world, which has undermined attempts to build a more sustainable, positive and hybrid peace and the expected gains that were to be made from a more cosmopolitan international society, furthered by a global civil society (Keane 1988, 21). The peacebuilding methods of the UN, EU, IFIs, INGOs, and their various programmes for security, peace and development have been significant for many of the world's conflict-affected citizens as in Bosnia, Timor, Northern Ireland or Colombia, but equally 'peace' has become a difficult concept for many people who have been subject to its processes, as with the Israel-Palestine conflict (Gonzalez-Vicente 2020).

This raises the problem of the relationship between intervention and peace-building: can intervention, in its attendant military, political, economic, and social dimensions be more effective if it is related to producing a higher quality peace, through new forms of governmentality that transcend the liberal governmentality of the peacebuilding era (e.g. digital governmentality)? Or does efficacy and thus legitimacy rest on limited, pragmatic, political goals for peace? Much of the policy documentation that has emerged over the last quarter of a century has been progressive in tone, but it has simultaneously emphasized the growing gap between intentions and outcomes. The realities on the ground span spoiling behaviour and blockages emerging from authoritarianism as with the Hun Sen regime in Cambodia, invasion and civil war as in Iraq, and softer but ineffective quasi-liberal and trusteeship-oriented regimes as in Bosnia (see Stedman 1997; Newman and Richmond 2006; de Oliveira 2011; Leroux-Martin 2014, 208; Bell and Pospisil 2017; Lewis, Heathershaw and Megoran 2018; Belloni 2020). Statebuilding is a contemporary form of counterinsurgency in some subtle ways (Richmond 2017, 48), which holds back claims for expanded rights in any peace process. This perhaps adds up to a substantial counter-peace framework, and digital tools could either offer a rebuttal or a confirmation of its path (Richmond 2020).

Clearly, digital approaches have potential for peacemaking in the light of such problems. A 'revolution in peacebuilding affairs' driven by the potential of digital peace would seek to compensate for the current lack of direct and indirect access for the UN, various internationals, donors, leading states, INGOs, in the world's conflict, emergency, revolutionary, and development areas. It also would need to compensate for the weakening of the legitimacy of the liberal peace/neoliberal state models and a loss of political will at the international level for new missions. Indeed, peacebuilding organizations have found digital platforms helpful to 'overcome logistical, financial and communication barriers that have traditionally impeded the effectiveness of peacebuilding programmes' (Peace Direct 2020, 20). For the UN, digital technologies are also seen as crucial for advancing the 'inclusion of a broader spectrum of views, including those of women and other groups tradition-ally excluded from peace processes, such as young people, minorities, indigenous communities and persons with disabilities' (UN General Assembly 2020, para 42).

They must also combat new types of political conflict emerging in the digital era, including the use of new technologies to fight wars, target civilians, suppress rights (cultural, economic and social as well as human rights): the exploitation of networks to support authoritarian regimes (such as using internet blackouts as part of the military's strategy to target and weaken opposition groups) (Gohdes 2015); to prevent the enhancement of extractive economies, and the heightening nationalist or populist politics (Owen 2015). Yet, many of these emerging problems, sometimes described as hybrid wars, relate to a rationality in which digital international relations mirror older geopolitics, leading to digital governmentality (drawing on surveillance capitalism) (Hoffman 2007). There is little or no coherent or plausible peacemaking response available from the UN, donors, NGOs, or national militaries as yet. In other words, violence in digital international relations may well be able to supersede the current, solely analogue capacity to make peace, leaving the critical project of an emancipatory form of peace no further forward even with its potential digital innovations (Richmond 2021). Yet, it is also clear that such innovations are necessary to be able to deal with the risks that digital and hybrid forms of violence have created.

Potential and Advantages

Digital international relations indicate a framework of intervention, diplomacy, and peace-oriented transactions that may thus be virtual, extremely fast, operate remotely and might be automated so access to networks and their control is absolutely crucial. This signifies the future potential and the current limits of 'digital peace'. It wavers between a connection with global justice in the future, where new knowledge and tools converge and facilitate the connection of the praxis of peace with justice and sustainability, and a status quo–oriented character in the present driven by geopolitics mitigated only slightly by the new micro-scale digital capacities. The latter appears to characterize the current situation, but it also suggests that there is potential that needs to be explored.

The activities associated with digital peacemaking may be coordinated by the traditional centres of power, including the UN Security Council Members, key states, and donors, or it may be devolved to digital, transitional civil society networks from 'enlightened' members of the UN Secretariat and donors. It may connect humans, states, institutions, companies, NGOs, and 'others', to networks and their expanded horizons and technologies. Thus, it may represent a significant shift in terms of peace, legitimacy, order, and power, away from territorial sovereignty and state authority structures. This suggests that digital peace contributions may have a substantial impact on traditional approaches to peacemaking, peacekeeping, mediation, peacebuilding, statebuilding, as well as international organization and the donor system, which are all state-centric and operate in analogue frameworks. This explains why UN agencies, donors, and various international actors have all become interested in digital potential for their various existing activities, and furthermore, in the question of how significant a change the digital terrain creates. It also indicates the close connection, and indeed evolutionary relationship between existing analogue approaches to peacemaking, and the new potential of digital approaches.

For example, broken infrastructures and blockages may be avoided through digital and technological advances, and local to international scales can be jumped (as with the use of new technologies in disaster relief, or for peace-keeping) (UN Secretary-General 2014). Since there is significant increase in the use of digital technologies by states, INGOs and transnational social movements, we can begin to piece together potential digital peace strategies currently available in the digital terrain of international relations, and measure them against the indications from the literature as to the necessary qualities of peacemaking in international relations and politics.

Digital Peacebuilding

Since the Cold War ended, peacebuilding has become one of the most innova-tive fields of international engagement for resolving and transforming conflicts (see Richmond and Visoka 2022). By its nature, peacebuilding requires creative solutions and methods to address the legacies and underlying conditions of conflict and to seek out innovative arrangements to promote peace, justice, and reconciliation. Part of this innovative mindset has long been the application and adaptation of ICTs as they emerged.

Lisa Schirch (2020) has identified five generations which capture the appli-cation of technology in peacebuilding activities. Initially, during the 1990s and early 2000s, the peacebuilding organizations used basic ICTs such as emails, websites, portals, and virtual communication platforms, such as Skype, to carry on their work and ease the communication and coordination between inter-national and local interlocutors, donors, and other stakeholders. Later on, during the 2000s and onwards a second generation emerged with the rise of smart-phones and 'web 2.0', whereby peacebuilding organizations adopted new ICTs to promote participatory and crowdsourcing methods of data collection, exam-ination, and dissemination, as well as using the Internet as a space for social mobilization and activism. During this time, 'peace tech' started to emerge as part of efforts to design tailored technological solutions for promoting peace. The third generation of the application of technology in peacebuilding context emerged in the early 2010s and related to the use of social media platforms to tackle the rise of hate speech, fake news, polarizations, and extremism. The fourth generation emerged in the late 2010s with the mobilization of civil society groups calling for the regulation of social media platforms to limit the spread of disinformation, harmful content, and negative social impacts. The fifth and latest generation concerns the rise of global digital movements to overcome and counter the use of technology for promoting authoritarianism and curtailing of human rights.

From all the generations of peacebuilding and technology, the second, third, and fifth generation appear to provide the richest grounds for scoping digital peacebuilding and its application in practice. In particular, the promise of digital technologies to enhance conflict analysis, expand the engagement with peacebuilding stakeholders, and promote pro-peace narratives and strategic, pluralist dialogue (Hirblinger 2020). The first and most common technological feature of digital peacebuilding includes the utilization of 'big data' in order to gather very large amounts of data at high speed from many sources, which may be useful for conflict mapping and analysis (Imran et al. 2018, 20). Big data are 'the vast amounts of digital data which are being produced in technologically and algorithmically mediated practices' (Richterich 2018, 2). They are characterized by a large volume of data generated through users of the Internet and social networking sites' digital interactions, which can be assembled and processed at a fast speed and often on real time, and can be collected in a broad range of varieties, as structured, semi-structured, or unstructured data. Big data are used for conflict forecasting and mapping the dynamics, actors, discourses, as well as documenting the audio-visual features of conflict and peace (Visoka 2016). The main tools which enable digital conflict analysis consist of text mining programs, news feeds, GIS tools, and other satellite imagery and visual mapping.

Of course, a substantial problem is that a significant amount of the data tends to be merely descriptive or trivial, and algorithms and interpretative processes may be biased towards external interests and ideology. They tend to overlook the fact that digitally collected data on conflict zones tend to suffer from omission errors which result from 'insufficient attention to or coverage of types, places, or periods of conflict'. When such omissions and bias are systematic, they can have 'deleterious effects' (Miller et al. 2022, 2). In other words, emancipatory structural change is unlikely even with digital peace developments, and prevention or prediction is mostly related to outside interests. Indeed, big data might actually be used to counter emancipatory processes, especially at the level of civil society, by elites, state, or international and hegemonic actors – especially considering the fact that these latter are the ones that possess the capability to develop and deploy such technological tools. Generally speaking, scholarship and policy reporting tend to accept the potential for digital approaches, and argue that peacebuilding is lagging far behind other areas.[13] It rarely examines the ethical and methodological risks, nor examines the possibility that the international political economy of digital

---

[13] 'Data for Peace & Security: Report of the Practitioners Workshop on Harvesting Best Practices and Building a Community of Practice' Govt. of Netherlands, NYU, & UN DPPA (July 2019): https://reliefweb.int/report/world/data-peace-security-report-practitioners-workshop-harvesting-best-practices-and.

peace may undermine subaltern claims. Peace is thus rendered a bureaucratic and technocratic process through these digital additions, which augment analogue approaches centred on territorial sovereignty and centralized power, rather than acknowledging political, local, and justice claims.

Media, Data, and Mobilization for Peacebuilding

Another strand of digital technology relevant for peacebuilding concerns the use of mobile technologies, virtual communication via Internet and social media platforms to promote inclusivity and deliver strategic messages. Social media platforms, short message service (SMS) systems, and online communications provide opportunities for conducting digital campaigns to promote peace agreements and reconciliation among conflict parties. Such campaigns have the potential to challenge the rumours and counter-peace narratives and promote alternative and shared narratives that could bring communities together. Charity organizations such as Peace Direct show that 'positive peace messaging on social media played an important role in instilling a desire for peaceful change in elections in Ghana and Liberia, and positive messaging around the contributions of youth have increased youth participation in peacebuilding' (Peace Direct 2020, 24). Platforms such as Zoom, Microsoft Teams and Google Meets are widely used as digital spaces for organizing problem-solving workshops, seminars, and conferences to promote exchange of views, story-telling, dialogue and joint endeavours among conflict parties.

Online platforms can also be used for promoting deliberative forms of peacebuilding and statebuilding, ranging from citizen inclusion and consultation in drafting peace agreements, constitutions, and vital laws governing political reforms and transition to sustainable peace. The reach can be much higher via digital platforms compared to transitional in-person peacebuilding trainings, seminars, and workshops (Peace Direct 2020, 13). In this sense, digital technologies are widely recognized as a tool in democratizing and decentralizing the scope and actors of peacebuilding endeavours. Examples from Afghanistan to the Democratic Republic of Congo show that marginalized groups such as women and youth have found a new role in the plural nature of digital technologies and thus increased their involvement and voice their needs in peace processes (Peace Direct 2020, 12). Sawa Shabab (Together Youth) is a South Sudan peace radio series aired by nearly thirty local stations across the country, which aims to promote 'peace and stability by empowering youth to be confident, open-minded, participatory citizens in a diverse society' (PeaceTech Lab 2022). Another initiative in South Sudan, Hagiga Wahid uses online platforms to reach out to South Sudanese communities, including those internally displaced and in refugee settlement in northern Uganda 'to dispel malicious rumours and misinformation which can contribute to intercommunal tensions and lead to violence' (Peace Direct 2020, 25).

Digital technologies and the big data that can be extracted from the content of social media platforms have to some degree enabled the emergence of bottom-up forms of knowledge sharing about war and peace, also allowing bottom-up dynamics and actors to be identified, however, without providing security guarantees. In particular, these types of digital technologies have become central to how contemporary regime change and counter-revolutions unfold, as well as in a peacebuilding context.

Digital citizen journalism and cyber witnessing have emerged as new forms of information production and dissemination, which might overcome the state and international ran media or official journalism. This changes the dynamics of what content, events, and forms of knowledge are made available to wider audiences and thus challenges the gatekeeping functions of traditional media, think-tanks, metropolitan civil society groups, and donor-oriented peacebuilding organizations. Such localized, yet globalized, forms of sharing content via digital platforms have changed how local conflicts, elections monitoring, protests and contentious politics are reported internationally.

Experiences from different parts of the world show that 'peacebuilders are crowdsourcing information and utilising mobile and satellite technologies for data collection, to map out detailed conflict trends and hotspots on the ground' (Peace Direct 2020, 7). Such evidence from the field shows that 'this has vastly improved early warnings systems, enabling systematic and near real-time data to be shared, which has greatly reduced the time needed for critical responses' (Peace Direct 2020, 7). Such potential is also recognized by the UN Secretary-General who considers that ' [g]reater use of data and statistical modelling tools can improve traditional analytical methods, potentially reducing bias, while helping with early warning and the detection of potential crises' (see UN General Assembly 2020, para 42). However, such applications tend to be reactive and address immediate problems rather than causal factors. This also reflects the character of the wider peace architecture, which is generally reactive and slow to respond (Richmond 2022).

For example, a widely popular example is the Ushahidi platform that maps crowdsourced data about disasters, elections, corruption, and political and domestic violence, which can be used for influencing political change.[14] In Sierra Leone, the efforts of the non-partisan National Election Watch to monitor the procedures of the 2007 presidential election via an SMS rapid-reporting

---

[14] See Ushahidi impact cases: www.ushahidi.com/in-action/case-studies.

system have been recognized as catalytic not just for the validation of results, but also in promoting a 'fair and peaceful election environment' and contributing to 'the peaceful transition to a new administration' (Schuler 2008, 143). The Kenyan case which gave birth to the Ushahidi platform has been used to collect crowdsourced data from a variety of media to visualize crises on an online map on a real-time basis. It has also been used to coordinate responses in the aftermath of Haiti's earthquake in 2010; in Niger's and Kenya's elections in 2011 and 2013, respectively; in Somalia's Afgooye corridor, home to 'the world's largest concentration of internally displaced people' (Beaumont 2010) in the Philippines during hurricane Haiyan; in Nepal's earthquake; in monitoring violence in Syria and the Central African Republic; and elsewhere (Hunt and Specht 2019, 2).

The value of real-time information (its speed, volume and variety) and the utility of its visualization helps explain the recent surge of interest in academic research on the potential of big data in the context of humanitarianism, peacebuilding and development (Karlsrud 2014; Read et al. 2016). Thus, for peacebuilding organizations, such as Peace Direct (2020, 6), 'digital technologies provide peacebuilders with user-friendly, efficient and scalable tools that not only improve programming and communications, but can also create alternative infrastructures for peace – challenging dominant conflict narratives and fostering positive communication and social cohesion between conflict groups'.

Conflict Analysis

This connects to another aspect of digital peace, drawing on new forms of conflict analysis. The analysis of peace and conflict dynamics at the social and local levels is an important component of conflict prevention and peacebuilding interventions. Over time several, digital conflict mapping and early warning platforms have emerged, such as Armed Conflict Location & Event Data Project (ACLED), which offer the potential of the visualization and datafication of conflict dynamics. It is argued that this is particularly useful for monitoring and the evaluation of peacebuilding projects and their wide social and political impacts. Peacebuilding research groups and institutes increasingly use Google Forms, Facebook, and other online media platforms for collecting conflict-related data as well as surveying public opinion on central issues prolonging the conflict and blocking peace. Platforms such as PeaceTech Lab established by the US Institute of Peace have partnered with local peacebuilding groups throughout Africa and the Middle East to develop digital tools for tracking hateful language and its role in promoting violence and undermining peacebuilding efforts. In the Middle East, the Yemen Peace Track Initiative has become a central platform for tracking the ceasefire negotiations, documenting hate speech, and engaging local women's groups in online consultations with the UN (International Alert 2020, 6).

The second type of digitally run technologies applied in conflict-affected settings concerns remote access, documentation, and intervention. Big data helps identify danger spots and their dynamics (early warning), as well as support networking via various forms of media in order to respond to them (a widely noted recent occurrence in the 'Arab Spring') (Karlsrud 2014). This is connected to the use of newish technology for surveillance, from satellites to drones (as used in a number of occurrences, as in 2015 to track the crashed Malaysian Airliner and Boko Haram). However, such large volumes of descriptive data tend to undermine the political and ethical claims being ascribed to peacemaking or peacebuilding, pushing its practices towards problem-solving rather than emancipation (Pugh 2005).

Remote Access in Conflict-Affected Environments

Access has been a major issue in conflict-affected regions, requiring political will as well as risk-taking, both of which are difficult to calibrate. Remote intervention using drones is already being used to engage in various ways (delivering supplies or expertise; for surveillance; pamphlet dropping; democratization; rule of law; gender mainstreaming; DDR; in-a-box kits – such as those RAND developed in the 2000s for statebuilding) in trouble spots, humanitarian emergencies, as well as in remote communities requiring support (hints of this development are to be found from Afghanistan to Nigeria today). 'Jumping' over broken infrastructures to reach victims has been made easier. More offensive forms of intervention may also be automated and connected to such new types of 'integrated missions', as with the military uses of drones and other technologies (Der Derian 2001). Such approaches probably require a mixture of military, political, humanitarian, and technological coordination and support in a relatively centralized manner. There are interesting possibilities in such emergent circumstances, but also there are (Orwellian style) dangers in them. There has been a tendency to see progressive potential (via the expansion of global civil society, resistance, and human rights for example), but new digital forms of governmentality can also be used to restrain the goals of peacebuilding towards a negative peace which is hard to legitimate locally, even if it maintains a regional balance of power.

Other significant forms of remote, digital peacebuilding consist of using GIS technologies for monitoring and mapping the situation on the ground and countering official narratives about the conflict and peace situation on the ground. While the UN has a sophisticated GIS system which is increasingly used in conflict mediation and peacebuilding context, there are other open-source and crowd-sourced tools, such as Global Incident Map or MDA Geospatial Services which provide low-cost alternatives to the official tools. Technological advances in satellite imaging, image processing capabilities, and surveillance technologies more generally, have a direct impact on some of the UN's core peace and security missions. The UN Security Council Resolution 1706 was the first that explicitly called for the use of 'aerial means' and 'aerial reconnaissance' by the UN Mission in Sudan (UNMIS) in an effort to help protect civilian populations (UN Security Council 2006).

Since then, drones have been used by the UN for the protection of refugees and internally displaced populations (IDPs) in Chad in 2009, and in 2013 their use was officially adopted by the organization for the support of its mission in Congo (MONUSCO) (BBC News 2013). The UN has also used drones in Haiti in 2010 to map disaster-stricken areas as well as to support the International Organization of Migration in its efforts to map sites of IDPs in 2012 (Karlsrud and Rosén 2013, 2). Drone and satellite imagery are also used by the UNDP to support the activities of humanitarian and development actors in Mali, and disaster preparedness and response in the Maldives and Tanzania (UN Development Program 2017). Finally, in MONUSCO's case, drones are not only used in their capacity to respond to violence but also as deterrents (UN News Center 2013).

In fact, the potential of this technology has led the DPKO's Expert Panel on Technology and Innovation in Peacekeeping to recommend its use as 'an immediate measure' (UN 2015c, 55). There are important questions here still unanswered, however. Who owns or leases the technology, who has access to it and the data it opens up, as well as the nature of the sub-contractual relations it often depends upon are open to question. Indeed, it appears that, despite the increased number of stakeholders and the inclusion of new, lower stratum actors such as everyday, local communities into the framework(s) of conflict resolution and peacebuilding/peacemaking, new dependencies are emerging with the adoption of such technologies. These increasingly resemble older power relations, thus perpetuating the characteristics and agendas of analogue international relations and peace, only this time with digital tools. All of the examples cited above indicate the valuable though politically limited goals of crisis management in humanitarian, emergency, or disaster responses, rather than an engagement with the political forces that drive conflict or the emancipatory political claims that emerge from conflict-affected societies through a political settlement inherent in peace processes, peacebuilding, and statebuilding. It is not coincidental that, despite the variety of technologies developed and deployed for the purposes of peace, no more progress has been made when compared to the old/analogue structure(s). This means ascribing political progress to digital tools may well be premature, even if basic needs and security are on their agenda.

Assessing Digital Peace

Clearly, questions of emancipatory agency are crucial in deciding the path that digital peace takes in the future, this being perhaps one of the longest-standing dynamics that has been noticed, particularly in constructivist work on human rights, post-structural work on identity and resistance, and interdisciplinary work on social movements and mobilization (Melucci 1989). Understanding 'digital interventions' would be necessary, including remote peacekeeping, and the use of drones in a variety of applications (from disaster relief to humanitarianism, via remote surveillance). The potential for monitoring and conflict prevention, anticipating causes and trends of conflict, humanitarian crises, and natural disasters using so-called big data is also crucial.[15] Digital diplomacy also offers potential, encompassing digital embassies, ambassadors, the use of social media, virtual summits, and other related forms of multilateralism (Fletcher 2016). Further dynamics include the digital recognition of states (and their potential exclusion). Hybrid forms of warfare are also connected to digital international relations (as in the Russian involvement in Crimea and Ukraine). Many other dimensions are opening up: humanitarianism and the use of e-payment for refugees; virtual terrorism and counter-terrorism conducted as 'marketing campaigns on the internet (often using, as with ISIS, violent images and videos); digital civil society, including digital protests, and internet-based resistance movements; digital forms of democracy such as the digital citizenship system in Estonia; questions about the right to the internet; the digital economy for services and exchange; and digital environmentalism.

Any progressive vision in digital international relations relating to peace, security, or development also has important methodological dimensions, which challenge older quantitative and qualitative approaches. Digital discourse analysis has become possible, with large-scale databases of peace-agreements, peace processes, diplomatic and official statements, and a related effort to quantify conflict, development, and peace indicators (Roberts et al. 2016). This is connected to the potential of digital ethnography and post-field research methods from digital humanities and social sciences, perhaps creating online databases of interviews and other qualitative data. On the other hand, so

---

[15] Very preliminary discussions have been taking place in UN institutions like PBSO, PBC, DPKO, and UNDP. Some reference has been made in UN SG briefings, as well as by various under-Secretary-Generals.

far, 'big data' and the re-quantification of research and policy methods appears to undermine the ethical premise of peace theories, replacing textured notions of emancipation with mass-produced conceptions of virtual self-help that are rarely plausible in war apart from at a very basic level, as in Syria.

Difficulties in Scale and Application, and Ethical Questions

In practice, the positive potential of peace in digital international relations has been limited by the inertia produced by the sheer scale of obstacles to peace underpinning analogue forms of international politics, including authoritarian power structures, a lack of political will, and regional geopolitics. The balance of power this denotes has effectively been maintained by formal, official, state-backed face-to-face diplomacy in complex multilateral public institutions like the UN, EU, OECD-DAC, and in national Parliaments. Military support or intervention, state, economic, and social programming by the UN, World Bank, donors and NGOs have been similarly unresponsive, as the tortured process of intervention and peacemaking in the Balkans since 1992 illustrates (Holbrooke 1998). Much of the analogue international peace architecture depends on static citizenship in territorialized sovereign states in order to enable rights, law, representation, and common international standards, but it is also underpinned by the balance of power and regional geopolitics.

This legacy architecture is clearly being heavily disrupted by these escalating digital dynamics, but rather than pushing the concept of peace towards a global justice framework as noted (see Lewis, et al. 2018), it still appears to be status quo oriented, leading to a re-emergence of quasi-authoritarian regimes around the world (et al. 2018). Indeed, this holding framework suggests an escalation towards violence is inherent in peace processes and peacebuilding that have become deadlocked or frozen over time (Smetana and Ludvik 2018). For interlocutors or participants in a broad range of activities aimed at peacemaking, this inevitably means the form of peace will follow suit: it will be negative, fragile, and always on the brink of escalation and collapse. Digital innovations have gone some way towards preventing further backsliding or the collapse of the peacebuilding framework (Haggard and Kaufman 2021). Some of these digital dynamics may appear to some degree to facilitate both social power and state capacity, and yet they also to marginalize the social and political, substituting neoliberalism, technology, capital, and technocracy as the basis for peace settlements (as can be seen with former US President Trump's ambiguous peace process in the Middle East) (Landau and Lehrs 2022).

In its early days many thinkers saw possibilities for progress, through social networks, communications and transport, global civil society, and technological advances which would bring to an end poverty, injustice, and instability (Scholte 2001; Kaldor 2003). However, older power structures and hierarchies have proven to be resilient despite the advent of expanded human rights, global epistemic networks, and their reform-oriented political consequences (as might be seen after the recent 'revolutions' across the MENA region) (Hinnebusch 2015). This can be seen in the breakdown of many extended peace processes recently (the Middle East, Syria, Sri Lanka, Colombia, Bosnia, Kosovo, and Cyprus to name a few) and the pressure on others (such as in Northern Ireland), the resurgence of authoritarian governments, and the wavering of the spread of democracy (according to Freedom House's data) (Freedom House 2017). The frameworks that countered war and violence in the analogue world, namely the rule of law, democracy, human rights, and international law and organization are now themselves being easily countered. No peace solutions have yet been found to the shift of power from the state constitution and international institutions to the market and global network defined by capital and technology. Digital (atmospheric) rather than liberal industrial power has not (yet) been reconciled with liberal peace or its as yet unknown successor (Richmond 2017, 2022). As with peacemaking in the context of the industrial-military states of the early twentieth century, peace in a digital context would have to stabilize the existing system's dysfunctionality and also deal with its new dynamics (Fukuyama 1988).

Conclusion

Under the conditions of digital international relations, peace may not be made between political units leading to legal or diplomatic agreements about the nature of a state and constitution, the sharing of power, the reorganization of boundaries, and the extension of rights and democracy as was claimed early on in the development of this literature (Zartman and Rasmussen 1997). Instead, it may often be about trying to find a way to accept a diminished (rather than augmented) and stratified space for humans in the world dominated by technology, speed, military applications, capital, and their related networks. It may mean reduced human rights and democracy, reduced states, and their safety nets, along with territorialism and borders which replicate elite interests (e.g. geopolitics and capital rather than cooperation and rights), and overall a reduced place for the material world and natural environment as international relations shifts into the techno-capitalist, geo-economic sphere, even over realist notions of geopolitics. Elements of these dynamics can be seen in the post-Cold War list of peace agreements that have gone awry, including in Cambodia where authoritarian rule favours extractive capital, in Colombia where a peace dividend was undermined by a refusal to negotiate over structural matters, or in Bosnia and

Kosovo where ethno-nationalism is manipulated by elites to maintain geopolitical and economic interests. In other words, there are serious scientific and ethical issues with the nature of peace that digital developments in IR imply, even despite the promise that such new tools and methods may carry.

Under the conditions of digital international relations, rights, sustainability, and democracy may be contested- or even displaced- via a struggle over access to networks and technology, as well as the crucial sources of energy needed to maintain these in the interests of elite (Tainter 1988). Enormous levels of complexity may actually heighten the risk of systemic collapse, while also endorsing the apparent need to develop ways of remotely operating and automating this system (nudging, intervention, etc.) (Thaler and Sunstein 2008). The space for global civil society that once appeared to be opening up with the emergence of new capacities and tools in order to support the growth of liberal internationalism, the UN system, rights, law, and free media, may end up being curtailed (Kaldor 2003; Visoka and Lemay-Hébert 2022). As concepts of peace and peacemaking shift onto digital platforms and networks a 'firewall' may well be created around political debate by the new power-holders who control access to networks and key nodes (Castells 2009). This means that politics, protest, and the expansion of rights is confined to virtual spaces, so it has little or no material impact on deeper structures or power-relations and power-sharing maintains the very stratifications that caused war in the first place (Richmond et al. 2021).

5 The Perils of Digital Peacebuilding

Introduction

The discussion in the previous section leads to more substantial concerns about the limitations of digital peace, which are ever present given the continuing scale of war and violence in international relations, and even when discussing its benefits (Richmond and Visoka 2021a). Critical versions of Digital IR perform a similar role as with the critique that was mounted against realism and liberalism in the so-called third and fourth debate (Lapid 1989). They interrogate its power relations, hierarchies, exclusions, and ethics, which indicate significant flaws in the commonly accepted understanding that digital IR is a platform for progress. Indeed, it seems that the mainstream versus critical theory binary of analogue forms of IR may well be transferred onto this emerging platform, expanding realist dynamics under the cover of digital frameworks, and offering new but extremely limited emancipatory modes of analysis or responses as camouflage. The epistemological tensions of analogue IR are being transferred, effectively, from one historical and theoretical epoch to the next, whilst also expanding the terrain of the debates into newer areas (e.g. networks, the Anthropocene, technology, etc). This means that the various peacemaking frameworks, in theory and practice that have sought support from these new developments need to advance cautiously. Historical power and hegemony may be reinventing themselves whilst rights claims advance only discursively but often not materially.

This section examines in more detail the risk that digital peace epistemology is susceptible to critique on the grounds of evading peace's connection to justice, legitimacy, sustainability, and reconciliation, will emerge mainly as a rhetorical or therapeutic, method in the practice, policy, or doctrinal frameworks of foreign policy, regional geopolitics, statebuilding, and stabilization. This points to the concept's potential ethical limitations vis-à-vis power-structures in international and domestic war, conflict, and violence.

A Fine Balance between Perils and Potential?

The next 'debate' on peace in IR, if it is indeed digital, may well – as argued earlier – be multi-scalar, transversal, mobile, and global justice-oriented, perhaps proceeding far away from the institutions of epistemic power (parliaments, international organizations, states, leading universities, key associations, etc.). Or it may be contained in a digital and virtual terrain of politics where it can have little material impact on the updated, geopolitical workings of international relations in practice (Der Derian 2001). The relationship between new technologies and the conduct of war, its remote and automated technologies, offers a different road towards peace than that offered by critical IR and its focus on rights, norms, and institutions, or more radical understandings of pluralism, justice, and sustainability: more a technologically dependent, automated and remote version of realism, facilitated by neoliberalism (Der Derian 2001). This provides a glimpse of what digital IR means for the construction of legitimate political authority after war. Authority would remain mainly rooted in elite power-structures (the state, political economy, the military–industrial/technological complex, warlords, and associated networks) (Zuboff 2019b), which exploit digital tools for access and control of populations, territory, borders, and power, whilst also engaging with the nexus between global neoliberal, military, authoritarian and technology networks (Biebricher 2020). Engagement with liberal norms and post-colonial arguments, law, democracy, justice, and rights, would at best be a cover for their co-optation.

This would imply rights and access to networks (such as donor networks, social movements, or global civil society) would be set by digital hegemons and driven by regional and geopolitical powers. This would mean that the quality of peace emerging from such foundations would operate at a very basic, and negative level, rather than the positive, hybrid, everyday, and justice-oriented models that critical scholarship and indeed UN doctrines suggest (UN 2018; Richmond 2022). Hegemony would therefore shift towards the control of access to networks, from civil society to the elite, state, technology, and global economy nexus. Peace tools, with their digital enhancements, would consolidate this system, which explains why so few policy documents and policy-oriented scholarship on digital and peace 'tech' tools are able to deal with the critical concerns of conflict-affected populations. Constitutional orders and their reform would be subservient to surveillance capital, which would also shape public opinion in conflict-affected societies (as it has elsewhere).

The engagement of peacemakers, the donor community, the international institutions involved in peacekeeping and peacebuilding would similarly be determined by digital geopolitics in which technologically enhanced political and economic power might displace existing political centres of legitimate authority (e.g. liberal societies, governments, and international actors). This would occur through traditional geopolitical means aimed at preserving the digital status quo, but also through networked encumbrances designed to prevent the further expansion of rights claims by conflict-affected subjects. This could be described as a 'counter-peace' framework (Pogodda et al. 2022) aimed at blocking the conceptual development of peace towards global justice, which has become apparent during the *longue duree* of its conceptual development (Richmond 2022). It returns the international system to geopolitical multipolarity, arms races, and other dynamics of escalation (Öniş and Kutlay 2020; Paris 2020; Jones and Marc 2021), as can be seen in recent Russian wars in Syria and Ukraine (among others) (Allan 2020), or Chinese harassment of Taiwan (Jütersonke et al. 2021), as well as western, NATO, and US responses, and the substantial marginalization of the UN (Stent 2022). None of the practices, from peacekeeping to peacebuilding and peace formation, that developed in analogue modernity to prevent or stop war, have made the transition to combat the dangers of digital IR dynamics in a comprehensive manner. In fact there has been substantial backsliding (Haggard and Kaufman 2021, 1–4) in the digital era, though they have begun to add technological knowledge, wider data ranges, and expertise to their existing systems (UN 2015b). Some energy has been put into beginning the thinking required, but mostly it has followed an analogue strategic and military rationality, however (Der Derian 2001).[16]

---

[16] Confidential Sources, Personal Interviews, UNDPKO, May 2018.

War and Justice

In contrast to inertia in the evolution of peace the very notion of war has shifted from interstate confrontations using military forms, to sub-state or regional ethnic conflicts, to territorial conflicts over land and resources, to liberal interventionism, to hybrid wars (Hoffman 2007*)*, and far beyond. This has effectively reinvented the structural aspects of war aimed at inflicting structural (and cultural) violence by erecting or enforcing unjustifiable global inequalities through digital governmentalities, in addition to the various forms of multipolar dynamics, as well as inequality long patrolled by authoritarian, liberal, and neoliberal governmentality. This may be aimed more broadly at disabling the critical shifts that have been occurring towards a system of peace as global justice (incorporating historical, distributive, gender, security, and environmental dynamics, amongst others), as might be glimpsed in UN's Sustainable Development Goals of 2015, or the later Sustaining Peace agenda (UN 2018). Structural forms of war, and their more subtle system of order maintenance – digital governmentality – enforces and maintains opposition to global justice, hybridity, and sustainability, whilst enabling analogue power-structures and hierarchies to recover, reform, and make the transition into the digital era intact (Duffield 2019, 9; Zuboff 2019b). It implies that the large-scale data, networked, nexus frameworks that appear to underpin digital peace are to be employed merely for fine-tuned, nineteenth-century style, balance of power and conflict management approaches, rather than the development of emancipatory peace. This means this is effectively a counter-revolutionary framework designed to oppose, retard, and neutralize the development of a rights-based international peace architecture since the mid-twentieth century (Pogodda 2020).

How might such forms of war be dealt with under these conditions of digital international relations? What shape would legitimate political authority, peace-building, statebuilding, mediation, peacekeeping, and conflict resolution take? A starting point, as we argued in the previous section, would be to begin to update the international peace architecture (comprising liberal constitutional order, international law, institutions and human rights; regional organization; diplomacy, peacekeeping, peacemaking, peacebuilding, and development) for digital conditions. These tools must be updated to be able to work against hybrid and structural wars, the shift of power to atmospheric networks, speed and the digital reframing of territorial sovereignty and related time and space, as well enhanced technological methods of violence. They must combat the undermining of human rights and democracy, as well as the legitimacy of global peace, security and order, but also must be able to address the expanded claims being made by global civil society through the concurrent emergence of critical digital forms of agency. This must especially encompass two key deficits of the old liberal analogue peace: firstly, the nexus between material inequality, injustice, and forms of discrimination across the international system (Held 2004; Piketty 2014) exposed by global civil and social networks, and, secondly, environmental sustainability under the epistemologies of the Anthropocene (Steffen et al. 2011; Arias-Maldonado 2013). Such arguments may be unfashionable among those calling for communitarian, populist, authoritarian, and parsimonious 'pragmatism' (Bellamy 2019, 16) but such inconsistency across time and space, not to mention societies, is undermining the current international peace architecture (Negroponte 2011; Belloni 2020, 81–204). Any peace it will produce will be limited to a balance of power, albeit finally tuned, or a victor's peace, in which much of the international community, norms, and rights, are excluded, as the situation in both Syria and Ukraine illustrate (Lewis et al. 2018). Digital legitimacy and authority rests in its critical version on meeting expanded claims for everyday rights in the context of justice and sustainability, as opposed to what currently appears to be the very substantial risk of the reconstitution of neo-feudal or elite power connected to geopolitics and geo-economics in the twenty-first century (Buzan and Lawson 2013).

Widening Interest versus More Grounded Application?

With the above caveats in mind, the potential and risks of technological innovation (both low- and high-tech) are increasingly being explored and investigated in less naive ways, for the purposes of facilitating, enabling and amplifying peace (Hattotuwa 2004, 51; Stauffacher et al. 2005; Mancini 2013; Karlsrud 2014; Sandvik et al. 2014; Morrison 2016). To date, research on the role of information and communication technologies (ICTs) has uncovered potential in the context of humanitarian relief (HICT), mid-term development (ICT4D), crisis prevention and early warning systems (Leaning and Meier 2009; Stauffacher et al. 2011), the monitoring of pre- and post-electoral violence, and the use of 'big data' for peacekeeping (Mac Ginty 2017). The fact that credible organizations, like the United States Institute of Peace, Harvard University and the Massachusetts Institute of Technology, were quick to engage in peace-related ICT research quickly attracted the UN's attention, which, in a 2015 report, noted the significance of new technologies both to the benefit of its missions as well as to 'the practical needs of end users on the ground' (UN 2015a). Yet, in the light of the above, such attention seems to be related to reducing goals, more efficiently achieved, reducing the prominence of human rights or a peace agreement down to the lesser level of conflict management.

On the one hand, NGOs are five times more likely to use new technologies to include more voices and provide alternative narratives across global networks, informed by wide-ranging comparative and innovative data and methods, in peacebuilding contexts than international governmental organizations (Gaskell et al. 2016, 6). And yet, they do not have the same level of resources, capital, and power, that states and elites may have. As noted by peacebuilding organizations on the ground, '[s]tructural barriers such as poverty, weak infrastructure and low digital literacy – critical enablers for socio-economic transformation – are preventing large segments of the global population from accessing digital technologies' (Peace Direct 2020, 7). Digital technologies have little as yet in the way of an answer for structural barriers to peacemaking, meaning that broadening data, efficiency, representation, and speed, cannot yet be seen as a significant response to structural obstacles or ethical questions, particularly related to limitations in the quality of peace (Wallensteen 2015).

Inequality and the Digital Subaltern

The newly emerging digital system does offer some potential for a more grounded and, more importantly, relational understanding of the very complex and wide varieties of experiences of violence and expectations for peace (Qin 2018). It amplifies the concerns and often the rights claims of subaltern and social actors and groups that may not have been heard in the older framework (Arendt 1951; Morton 2007; Bailliet and Larsen 2015; DeGooyer et al. 2018, 4). Yet, unequal access to digital platforms tends to affect mostly marginalized groups and minorities, meaning that they may also be more exposed to bias or digital forms of governmentality. Evidence from the field shows that digital peacebuilding efforts are often gender-blind and tend to have adverse effects on marginalized groups. As Louise Arimatsu shows, digital platforms often 'reproduce, and often amplify, the patriarchal structures, practices, and culture of contemporary life' (Arimatsu 2019). International Alert notes that in many parts of the world '[w]omen continue to face political, financial, technical, and cultural barriers that prevent them from using ICTs effectively for greater inclusion in conflict prevention and peacebuilding' (International Alert 2020, 2).

ICTs are not a panacea for the deficiencies of bureaucratic-led, liberal peacebuilding, in other words (Tellidis and Kappler 2016; Mac Ginty 2017; Miklian and Hoelscher 2017). ICTs can foment (and indeed accelerate) exclusion and authoritarianism as much as they can facilitate inclusion and accountability (Morozov 2011; Rød and Weidmann 2015). They are often unregulated or market-driven. Similarly, they can instigate or help sustain violence as much as they can be drivers of dialogue and non-violent mobilization (Bailard 2015; Warren 2015).

Tiberiu Dragu and Yonatan Lupu argue that 'without denying the beneficial effects of digital technologies to opposition groups, many argue that technological advancements also empower authoritarian governments by facilitating preventive repression' (Dragu and Lupu 2021, 996). They define preventive repression as 'a wide range of tactics aimed at identifying, monitoring, and tracking potential regime opponents so as to neutralize them before they pose any real threat to the government' (Dragu and Lupu 2021, 993). Furthermore, ICTs encourage innovative methodologies but access issues also mean they risk creating peacebuilding's 'digital subaltern'. As Tellidis and Kappler (2016) have noted, there is a risk that ICTs may be co-opted by international and donor organizations and institutions, so as to manipulate data, disguise or neutralize the real consequences of interventions, and/or be treated as yet another tool for the imposition of externalized peacebuilding, aid and development agendas connected to hegemonic interests (see also Hurwitz 2014; Muller 2015).

The assumption that digital international relations are a venue for expanded rights claims through the smooth interconnection between claimants and facilities is further undermined by the probability that without mediation, communication and politics reflect existing stereotypes and indeed power relations. Inequalities of various sorts continue to underpin digital international relations, and by extension, determine the limits of digital capacities in peacemaking and peacebuilding. As an extension of liberal peacebuilding capacity, it also lacks local legitimacy, as digital IR and digital approaches to peacebuilding offer vertical relationality across power relations from local to global, but those power relations still remain. At the same time, it could well extend the power of key actors in more traditional notions of IR, including key institutions, the military, non-state violent and criminal actors, and extractive capital. As noted by peacebuilding organizations, such as International Alert, 'in addition to the challenges raised above, issues of elite capture continue to present challenges to the peacebuilding sector as it adapts to the online realities' (International Alert 2020, 7). International Alert further notes that 'a rapid desk review on digital consultations found a bias towards inviting contributions from what are often referred to as "expert-level" participants, such as INGOs, governmental and multilateral-level actors, rather than "community-level" participants, or grassroots local community constituencies, again leading to the silencing of marginalised voices, including civil society actors'. (International Alert 2020, 7).

Lessons Learned and Digital Governmentality

Thus, the digital framework may equally lead to new forms of digital governmentality which reflect and support older power structures associated with the state, metropolitan NGOs, business groups, or the military. In sum, as with previous versions of peacebuilding, there are three plausible paths for 'digital peacebuilding'. Firstly, it may support the neo/liberal peace, and states-system that has emerged, placing security, trade, and technology slightly but significantly over expanded rights and critical understandings of peace and emancipation. Secondly, it may extend the dynamics that lead to war and violence even further, as is evident in the voluntary and non-binding character of cyber-norms initiated by the UN (Tikk 2018). Thirdly, it may connect with, but moderate expanded social claims for rights and global justice. It takes the neoliberal version of peace associated with statebuilding and stabilization approaches (a form of digital, neoliberal governmentality) (Clausen and Albrecht 2021) as a plausible response to the post-9/11 extension of the means of violence into hybrid war terrains as the contemporary form of conflict that an emancipatory version of the digital peace must now respond to (Freire and Simão 2021, 202).

These developments raise a number of issues and problems. Primarily it fails to learn the lessons of the last thirty years that rights, material needs, and root causes, have to be dealt with in ethical ways that are acceptable to conflict-affected societies. This requires structural reform rather than merely the digital finessing of analogue forms of peacebuilding. Furthermore, there are multiple sites of legitimate authority engaged in peacemaking with overlapping constituencies. Under networked approaches to sovereignty, legitimacy is networked, scalar, and mobile, rather than territorially fixed to centralized institutions. Instead of building legitimacy, this digital peacebuilding revolution may build more efficient interventions and technological forms of territorial and centralized neo-trusteeship, effectively producing digital forms of governmentality of limited substance for those interested in positive, hybrid, and everyday forms of peace connected to expanded rights, sustainability, and understandings of global justice (Richmond 2021).[17]

On the other hand, this potential revolution in peacebuilding affairs could represent a new, technological turn that can be used to build a better security and peace framework, focused the localized and micro steps forward in the context of stabilization strategies (Krause 2019), while maintain future potential for areas such as human rights, gender equality, post-conflict justice, and others. However, as with liberal peacebuilding this development also represents opportunities for linkages with fluctuating foreign policy, strategic, economic, or ideological objectives on the part of hegemonic actors involved in peacebuilding. Even if the technological turn bypasses older conceptions of sovereignty, or

---

[17] See Goal 16 of the UN Sustainable Development Goals NY: UN (2015), www.un.org/sustaina bledevelopment/peace-justice/.

reinvigorates liberal peacebuilding, it still will not easily navigate the problem of local consent, the global ethics of peace, justice, and sustainability, the rise of networks, the existence of multiple sites of legitimate authority, and the need to engage with hybrid forms of peace which are emerging from international to local scale encounters. In particular, as Peace Direct (2020, 39) reports, '[g]overnment restrictions, including the taxing of social media and sites being blocked in some countries, create problems for peacebuilders in promoting their peace messaging around the world'.

There are likely to be two main perspectives on this: a practical evaluation of how to achieve renewed and improved access and 'rights of intervention' to support the expanded rights of conflict-affected communities for policymakers, donors, western militaries, the UN, and humanitarians; and, secondly, a normative/theoretical evaluation of the pros and cons for academics, peace actors, and internationals, possibly pointing towards issues of local legitimacy and global justice. However, restoring and improving access or the international right of intervention for protection of humanitarian purposes (for example, further building on R2P) seems implausible. As we have argued earlier, digital capacities offer insignificant assistance here and mainly are able to help with the gathering of data and the improvement of communications, and so structural and practical constraints risk undermining the local and international legitimacy of peacemaking and peacebuilding. The wider milieu of digital IR suggests ICTs may assist in conflict resolution through improved contact and data in micro-context, or humanitarian situations, but do little to alleviate the structural problems associated with state capture or failure, the growing multipolarity of the international system, and the nexus between insurgency, terrorism, and other forms of political violence, as well as hybrid wars.

Whereas the revolution in military affairs in the 1990s (Freedman 1998) led to US-derived counter-insurgency doctrines and UK military interest in 'stabilization' missions (Farrell and Gordon 2019) in places such as Afghanistan in the 2000s in order to support new forms of trusteeship and 'native administration' which were closely connected to analogue epistemologies of peacebuilding and statebuilding (Woodward 2017) the digital revolution in peacebuilding affairs would have to contend with problems of access, political and social legitimacy, claims for historic and distributive justice, and far more intense claims upon the state and the international system from conflict, emergency, or development-affected citizens than ever before. The opening up of communication across conflict lines, the creating of a broader, global, regional and local perspective through new digital networks, the improvement of access, the increase in mobility and reach of conflict-affected subjects, as well as peacemaking and peacebuilding actors, ensured this dynamics of expanding rights claims.

It would have to re-engage with an emphasis on global and distributive justice across geography and history in broad terms (O'Neill 2000, 115–42; Nagel 2005; Pogge 2005; Risse 2005), via a far more networked, mobile, decentralized, and complex framework, as well as demands for more egalitarian and representative forms of peace, the state, and the international. As Rawls has argued, any perpetuated inequality or injustice maintained by the state or the international would have to be clearly justified and acceptable to the general population, if indeed exceptions can be made under progressive and hybrid forms of positive peace (Rawls 1993). The boundaries of sovereignty in a digital, networked, and mobile world, could no longer be used to provide security, or implicitly justify internal and international inequality through constrained human rights, humanitarian or international law, as they are under realist or liberal modes of analysis, in other words. These contradictory dynamics of enhanced conceptualizations of peace in digital IR, while simultaneously reinforcing more traditional forms of power, has placed the contemporary international system and its peace tools under great stress.

As discussed in the previous section, the digital realm harbours and favours decentralization and, in certain cases, at least, supports democratization. Its ontology is based on disruption and networked (as opposed to social) relationality rather than centralization and universalization, which emphasizes the transmission of expert knowledge (Owen 2015). This has significant implications for the nature, role and future of states, international organizations and, ultimately, their various *modi operandi*. All of the examples cited in this study – ranging from digital conflict analysis to expanding inclusion and advancing strategic communication, data, access, or reach – indicate the valuable though politically limited goals of crisis management in peace oriented responses, rather than an engagement with the political forces that drive conflict or the emancipatory political claims that emerge from conflict-affected societies through a political settlement inherent in peace processes, peacebuilding, and statebuilding. This means ascribing potential for political progress to digital tools may well be premature even if basic needs and security are being addressed.

What we may actually be seeing on the horizon of international relations and its essential peace tools that maintain international and local order, are micro and local impacts, which add up to a wider picture of pacification without addressing root causes. This pacification process tends to contribute to the interests of the controllers of data processing capacities, owners of new technologies and networks, and to elites that have interpenetrates the state and global economy and carry such capacity over into peacemaking. Peacemaking and peacebuilding in this sense represents digital govenmentality which builds on hegemony and geopolitics, and limited peace tools to very basic and negative versions and operate in favour of great power and major economic, geopolitical/geo-economic interests (Buzan 2014; Buzan and Lawson 2014).

Problems in Practice, Underlying Structural, and Ethical Deficits

Such dynamics infuse many aspects of what it often identified as digital potential in literatures, doctrines and policy reports on peacekeeping and peacebuilding, mediation, conflict resolution or transformation, humanitarianism and development, which are all affected by such core limitations. For example, citizen journalism critiques and delegitimizes official/hegemonic narratives and discourses about particular conflict situations or crises. The broader dissemination of such texts, and their comparative weight across global networks, may well influence international policy but this also depends on the political will for peacebuilding at this level if deeper reforms are to be realistic. Opposing, more traditional media organizations control far resources, and the same tools, however.

Further examples with conflicting potential include the creation of platforms that have been developed as a response to the authorities' mass surveillance schemes (for instance, the Telegram app) as well as the surge in the creation of electronic (or 'crypto'-) currencies. Blockchain (the technology behind electronic currencies that allows for trustless, transparent, decentralized and unfalsifiable contracts between two parties) is something that has attracted the interest of various UN agencies: the World Food Programme has utilized the technology to authenticate and record food and cash transfers to vulnerable populations in Pakistan and Jordan (World Food Programme 2017), while the UN Office for Project Services (UNOPS) and the Office of Information and Communication Technologies (UN-OICT) are aiming to implement it to combat child trafficking by providing identities to undocumented children (World Identity Network 2017). UNICEF recently began recruiting gamers to mine the Ether cryptocurrency in aid of Syrian children and announced that it will be accepting donations in Bitcoin and Ether cryptocurrencies, which it will not convert to conventional currency. Others have also suggested that the technology can also help finance the organization's SDGs by doing away with the need to rely on charities, moral imperatives and ethical commitments (Brunnhuber 2018). Another way of looking at this would that peacemaking such a basis would shift further away from legitimate political claims within conflict-affected societies and more towards the interests carried through an uneven science, technology, capitalism, and geopolitics. Of course, control of a money supply is one of the foundations of sovereignty (along with the control of territory and taxation) so such moves would be controversial in that they undermine the state and presage global governance in which political economy is dominant rather than norms associated with rights and their expansion. Again, at present such digital prospects offer mostly ameliorative potential rather than supporting an emancipatory peace project, however, which suggests limited potential albeit in which the ethical and scholarly work on emancipatory notions of peace are less significant than elite or state interests.

Decentralization and disruption- commonly associated with digital dislocations of analogue IR- are not merely aimed at critiquing, removing or reforming oppressive and unjust power structures, however, but also are reactions to the settled norms and consensus that were once have been taken as leading examples of good practice under the post-Cold War liberal peacebuilding system. The digital dynamic mobilizes civil society and other actors, partly because it is not regulated by formal authorities or the state (although state control has proven easily to achieve), but on the other hand it pushes authority (if not legitimacy) towards those that control the networks in use. Power relations may thus remain unchanged, despite the early promise of decentralization (particularly where hegemony takes control of popular discourse as has recently been the case with the return of nationalism as a global political force). Counter-critique may indeed be used to disrupt peacebuilding even where it has an emancipatory goal as case after case has suggested more recently (Subedi 2021). Somewhat problematically, this implies that peacebuilding has become subject to the same contradiction between new tools to be applied to achieve practical progress and more regressive or merely ameliorative applications of digital governmentality, with concurrent ethical deficits. It is important to be wary about the risk that digital applications are used to undermine political reforms that are required to bring about a just and emancipatory peace, merely responding superficially to the symptoms of conflict. This problem appears to be no different under digital versions of peacemaking as it was under analogue versions (Hughes and Pupavac 2005; Pugh 2005).

From a northern epistemological perspective, multiple cyber-threats may arise from actors (mainly, but not exclusively, non-state) based in countries of the Global South, primarily because in those settings 'the introduction of technology has often outpaced the establishment of state institutions, legal regulations, and other mechanisms that could manage the new challenges arising from this technology (Schia 2018, 824). Recognizing this, the UN has attempted to strengthen cybersecurity capacity building (UN 2015b) in these countries aiming to protect the advanced economies and societies of the Global North, but also to support the economic development and socio-political stability that countries of the Global South may reap from digital technology's advances. However, as benevolent as this sounds, it does not eliminate the risk of imbrication in new systems of domination (Muller 2015). Indeed, as Hurwitz has argued, advanced states may lead their developing partners to focus on threats and risks that are of more concern to the former than to the latter (Hurwitz 2014, 330). Thus, from a post-colonial perspective, digital perspectives on peace and war simply accentuate dominant interests and seek to pacify new rights claims in and from the global south.

Clearly, ICTs do not offer a holistic remedy to peacebuilding's and statebuilding's recent problems. They are often difficult to regulate and often dependent upon private sources of capital and technology in the hands of elites with geopolitical and geo-economic framing, with little interest in new approaches and thinking about peace. As highlighted by the UN Secretary-General in 2020, 'social media have also helped to accelerate the spread of harmful content, including misinformation, hate speech and incitement to violence, often particularly targeting women, facilitated by algorithms and business models that prioritize viral content' (UN General Assembly 2020, para 43). They have generally worked in the interests of conservative and authoritarian elites, for whom nationalism, territorial sovereignty, and regional domination remain the goal regardless of whether they depending of the use of force or violence. For every benign use there exist numerous destructive others so far ungoverned and unregulated. The aforementioned example of the Telegram app and its use by ISIS (and other criminal groups) is one such case where the digital realm may jeopardize peacebuilding or conflict transformation processes and procedures. This risk is magnified when coupled with, perhaps, the biggest risks facing the UN: as the Expert Panel on technology and innovation in Peacekeeping highlighted, peacekeeping missions frequently lack the range of capabilities that other militaries and international organizations consider necessary to operate effectively (UN 2015c, 17; Dorn 2016). Slow adoption, therefore, means there are a large number of civilians that could have been protected, but were not.

Furthermore, 'digital technologies have intensified the tensions between security and law' (Aradau 2017, 329): judicial decisions and legal knowledge increasingly rest on anticipated future threats rather than evidence and/or proof of intention. The result of this is the normalization of the legitimacy of threats (perceived, constructed or actual), as well as the technological means that are promoted for countering said threats. Linking development and aid to the promotion and enhancement of digital connectivity without prior recognition of the significance of analogue needs or political and emancipatory claims (for example, electricity, education, rights, and legislation) (Schia 2018), undermines both the development efforts in these countries as well as the security frameworks necessary for all. As has been shown elsewhere, ICTs cannot guarantee political change or economic growth unless overseen by functional institutions and regulatory frameworks (Avgerou 2003). It could be argued that such administrative capacity, however, may be introduced (where it is lacking) or enhanced (where it exists but is not fully implemented) by peacekeeping and peacebuilding missions' ICT use in reforming, rebuilding and reconnecting society and the state to broader emancipatory goals. This could spur initial growth of the demand for ICT infrastructure, regulation, and policy – thus having macro-economic effects on the national economy, rather than simply the local economies around peacekeeping bases (Martin-Shields and Bodanac 2018). Yet, enormous political will and capital would be required, not to mention expertise, as well as checks and balances. Digital perspectives on peace point to international structural change and reform, but digital tools so far in practice provide only marginal and micro-level applications. This is a significant problem in the attempt to improve peacemaking with such capacities and also a challenge to recognize current limitations and to do better.

Digital peacebuilding raises also significant security and safety concerns, especially if online interactions are monitored by counter-peace groups. Such breaches of privacy and misuse of the online content can undermine the safety of peacebuilders, their ability to engage in genuine dialogue and express freely their views and position on sensitive matters. As mentioned above, the use of drones and other surveillance technologies by the UN also raises questions about the data privacy of the non-combatants that are being recorded. As Larauri and Meier (2015, 12) have noted, records of this information will most likely outlast the life of the mission, in which case no guarantees can be provided about the extension of 'do-no-harm' policies. Furthermore, surveillance technologies are perceived as tools for power and control, thus raising concerns about sovereignty and rights. In other words, digital peacebuilding is still embryonic, lacks emancipatory goals connected to subaltern political claims, and without legal and ethical regulation it risks becoming a form of digital governmentality harnessed by political hegemony.

The trade-off between privacy and data quality is also relevant to the evaluation of the usefulness of 'big data' (Imran et al. 2018). The way(s) in which data is being gathered and used are of paramount importance, particularly in authoritarian settings where the authorities would be very keen to know the identities of those submitting information about, say, violations of human rights. In Mexico, for instance, crowdsourcing for crime reporting led to drug cartels identifying and lynching participants (Monroy-Hernández et al. 2012). Furthermore, the greatest challenge is the sheer volume of information gathered as well as 'the ability/inability to sift through this information, verify it, confirm it, structure it and present it in a comprehensible manner, real-time' (Karlsrud

2014, 11). More critically, however, one must not exaggerate the ability of 'big data' to generate knowledge and intelligence that 'were previously impossible' (Boyd and Kate Crawford 2012, 663), particularly in conflict-affected regions where access to technology is still a privilege enjoyed by a few (et al. 2016). In other words, beyond the ameliorative and basic requirements of emergency and disaster relief, the digital augmentation of peacebuilding assists in expressing subaltern political claims and building a case for them (if it can overcome the problems of technological bias towards the interests of advanced societies and economies), but has little to offer for their implementation. Moreover, 'despite relative advantages in the speed and volume of data collection, automated approaches are vulnerable to trade-offs in the accuracy of the data collected, often encompassing errors in geographies, actors, timelines, and targets' (Miller et al. 2022, 2).

Datafication (Markland 2022) does not necessarily imply a better form of peace, nor does algorithmic bias, nor remote application, micro-applications, nor speed, networks, wider inclusion, bypassing state or elite power, that is unless an emancipatory, sustainable, and just political project can be more easily agreed upon with such new tools and capacities. So far positive evidence is lacking beyond small-scale applications and wider aspirations, and problems abound.

Conclusion

The logic of the application of digital technologies for peacebuilding has been mostly essentialist, namely assuming that the digital turn and technological progress is unstoppable and that it is imperative that peacebuilding organizations must adapt to such a technological progress. Technology is seen as a necessity and many actors naively accept the logic of digitality is outside human control, complies with bureaucratic, and legalistic rationalities and bypasses problematic political authority as well as difficult questions of legitimacy. This runs against the whole history of peacemaking, which shows that inclusion, legitimacy, and justice are central, and power or technology-centred approaches will eventually break down or be overturned because of a lack of legitimacy and sustainability (Richmond 2022). There are thus contradictory possibilities of ensuring that the digital and the social (human development) correspond to one another or accelerated alienation and exclusion. Much of the debate about new technologies, tools, and networks in framing peace thus rests on producing bureaucratic, legalistic, and apolitical engagements that do not do justice to subaltern political claims for a peace with rights, justice, and sustainability, nor recognize the intimate relationship between power, knowledge, and technology. They are thus framed by descriptive or resilience thinking in bureaucratic and technocratic modes. Consequently, they risk actually undermining the emancipatory endeavours of peacebuilding at a political level, even if they facilitate the access and reach of international actors seeking to pacify or respond to crises or the networks of local and civil actors. If anything, the range of digital activities surrounding peacebuilding further accentuates the growing gulf between its emancipatory claims and its limited, therapeutic praxis.

6 Conclusion

Pros and Cons: Changing Political Environments Yet Limited Peace Responses

Digital IR represents the latest layer of international relations, built upon a series of other historical frameworks, consisting of war and conflict dynamics and their related peace management and settlement systems. As we have seen, there are multiple, embedded, 'sticky', and 'co-produced' techno-sociological strands, techno-capitalist strands, techno-state, and techno-internationalist strands. They are increasingly entangled in peacemaking, peacekeeping, and peacebuilding, and differ in terms of their ethical capacities, practical qualities, and power-capacities (Hirblinger et al. 2022). There have been both naive and now more mature ambitions for digital peace, but they remain ambitions, in some cases propaganda, and in many cases naive. The focus on technological solutions, whether positive or pessimistic (Hirblinger et al. 2022), has been depoliticizing, and something of a distraction from the need for structural reform in peacemaking to a large degree.

Yet, elements of digital peace may predate the current technologies available but the digital element has also proved new impetus, speed, and reach to networks in international relations of old. It has offered the possibility of new solutions to old problems, but also the illusion of separation from those older problems. It is driving substantial structural change, perhaps making the territorial 'international' less significant in the face of various negative and positive global networks and their tools, which as yet unevenly balance limited peacemaking tools with substantial additions to war-making capacities. Digital peacemaking frameworks may propagate expanded rights and strengthen the international peace architecture or they may foreground more compromised neoliberal (Zuboff 2019b, 9) or disruptive technological and governmental power (Chandler 2018, 159). This is a major shift beyond the older geopolitical, industrial, and liberal–international version of IR (the analogue version of the Holocene, in other words). Networks and datafication may amplify power and resistance, and open up alternative dimensions of international relations, but they also enforce existing power relations and hierarchies through digital governmentality and new forms of atmospheric power (variously termed surveillance capital or digital governmentality).

Digital contributions to peace and to peacebuilding have clearly developed significant potential across a range of research, policy, and practice arenas. However in practice, their contribution is mainly at the micro-level in scale, and seems to be most potent under the control of more powerful actors at the macro-level, which actually may seek to subvert peacemaking or oppose it completely. Their deployment amongst social movements, NGOs, UN actors, mediators, peacekeepers, diplomats, and development actors, may facilitate existing peace practices but do not overcome their major structural weaknesses. They operate within existing structures and within geopolitics, which is increasingly multi-polar and is shifting away from norms and rights associated with critical and recent scholarship on peace. This suggests that digital peacemaking tools and theories have not yet caught up with the disruption and new capacities that digital IR offers for powerful actors in IR. This concern is substantial, and may also point to the fact that peacemaking never will be able to catch up with the potential for war and violence that has emerged in this terrain.

Even so digital developments in peacemaking, carefully handled, have the potential to contribute to the evolving international peace architecture, which is a palimpsest where these often contradictory past and legacy sediments are all visible at once. It represents a contradictory struggle to both break free of moribund peace systems and extend them to combat new forms of violence. As the latest layer, the digital framework for peace remains weak, however, given the tools for conflict that are present and enormously amplified by new technologies. Given the tools for mitigating their clashes and contradictions are far from commensurate, as this study has shown, far more work is required on the potential of digital developments from practical, methodological, as well as ethical perspectives.

Undoubtedly, digital peacebuilding has expanded the potential of peace building, from its original meaning which captured both international and local dynamics and approaches, and foregrounded subaltern claims against weak and authoritarian states, as well as a Eurocentric international community. It has opened up new questions relating to networks, data, access, surveillance, justice and ethics in the techno-spatial blending of offline and online modes of peace. In this sense, digital peacebuilding may represent the latest attempt to push for greater involvement of local actors and knowledge while retaining the dominant role for international peacebuilders, perhaps even more remotely. In other words, without foregrounding ethical issues, justice, and sustainability (as laid out in the UN's Sustaining Peace agenda) (UN Secretary-General 2018, para 6), it mainly refines or augments older practices. These dilemmas notwith-standing, digital peacebuilding could well contribute to representing new ways of thinking and acting in conflict-affected environments, which bypass the blockages and wider counter-peace dynamics, whilst pursuing context-specific emancipatory goals. So, digital peacebuilding platforms – as one area of digital international relations – have helped marginal political claims to become more prominent, but there is little evidence as yet that have produced substantial responses in practice. Digital peace praxis perhaps represents a move towards new terrains before the problems of the older 'analogue' order have been settled or resolved.

Digital peacebuilding is thus not a panacea for the old analogue order, though it appears to offer the key potential of enabling a transcendence of some existing barriers to peace (including problems related to positionality, locality, territori-ality and sovereignty, access to resources, technology and networks). Nor do digital approaches unproblematically empower subaltern emancipatory claims over digital forms of governmentality in practice, though has made marginal actors and positions more likely to be heard. Localized and networked attempts to identify ways to use such technologies in order to (re)claim agency and expand rights have been met with significant resistance by the old analogue, hierarchical, geopolitical, and territorial international order, on the other hand. As much as digital technologies have opened some new avenues for peace-building, they have been quickly co-opted and utilized by governments and ethnic entrepreneurs to curtail human rights and prevent peace and reconcili-ation in divided societies. There is a risk that although peacebuilding advocacy groups have, for example, called for governments and international organiza-tions to 'promote digital literacy and e-governance programmes to support digital inclusion in online spaces and in tech-based peacebuilding activities', we are likely to see more digital governmentality than digital peace in the foreseeable future (Peace Direct 2020, 8).

Moreover, while in theory digital approaches to peace may appear to offer the potential to predict and analyse conflicts, in practice such endeavours risk shifting peace and security processes to a technical level of analysis and engagement. Consequently, overreliance on digital solutions risks ignoring the underlying and fundamental political compromises involved in peacebuild-ing engagements. In fact, many peacekeeping and peacebuilding interventions have suffered from cultural biases against local populations, on top of their very limited resources and limited or fragmented political will. Technologies operat-ing on algorithmic formulas might in reality antagonize further and discriminate against certain targeted groups and local communities. The UN also admits that 'gender biases in machine learning models and data also run the risk of reinforcing stereotypes and locking in biases for the future' (UN General Assembly 2020, para 42). Indeed, experience about the use of technology and big data for counterterrorism, surveillance, and migration control illustrates how racialized and depoliticizing algorithmic predictions can be (Gilman and Baker 2014). Yet, these are underlying factors in most conflicts, meaning such tools may actually exacerbate existing conflict dynamics: conflict-inducing as opposed to peacemaking tools, in other words, given the massive imbalance between digital support for older structures of power and the agency it may offer to social movements.

Concluding Thoughts

Given these substantial deficits, it is difficult to see how digital humanitarianism and prevention, remote peacekeeping, and digital enhancements for peacebuilding or peacemaking might address the existing flaws in predicting, understanding, and responding to conflict trends; in creating suitable responses that carry local and regional legitimacy; and in amassing sufficient resources and political will to produce a peace dividend (Jacobsen 2015). By ignoring long-standing issues, particularly those raised by more critical appraisals of the theory and practice of peace in IR (Richmond et al. 2016; Richmond and Visoka 2021b), they risk deepening the insecurity of civilian populations in conflict. Moreover, the lack of technological resources and capacity to engage with new technologies in conflict-affected zones makes it extremely difficult for conflict-affected communities to make use of and benefit from such data and related tools. Essentially, these approaches might lead to a new form of 'digital colonialism' and 'digital trusteeship' that reproduces yet again the dynamics of material and cultural domination and exploitation within peace processes rather than responding to them as causal factors in war (Kwet 2019). So far they have not provided answers to the political claims, security or material problems of conflict-affected populations, as in Syria, Yemen, Ukraine, Myanmar, or many earlier conflicts where peace processes, mediation attempts, peacekeeping, diplomacy, or peacebuilding are now frozen or in retreat, such as in Cyprus, the Balkans, DRC, or Colombia.

Digital approaches give an impression of international engagement, but they offer little political substance in addressing the root causes and contemporary dynamics of the conflict than existing tools do. They augment rather than resolve, at least so far. They may even create the problematic impression that local communities are 'resilient' and can cope with war and political violence alone (Chandler 2014). They may actually distract from and reduce the possibility for engaged interactions between local and international actors and thus risk undermining the legitimacy of any externally and remotely designed or imposed peace settlement. Existing research shows that generating data, methods, and theory from a substantial distance about the local dynamics of conflict and citizens' perceptions on the ground is an unreliable approach to peace and security issues. Predictive systems and AI effectively operate on the symptoms of violence, and from a great methodological distance, rather than the causes or rights claims of conflict-affected societies.

The major lacunae in peacemaking activities so far have been a lack of political will for reform or intervention at state levels, and an absent political engagement with everyday, local political claims, rather than a lack of data or digital capacity, in actually fact. Take the Syrian war as an example. The availability of early warning capacity, data collection, and prevention technologies have been of no consequence in preventing or resolving it. Several rounds of UN mediation have failed even though such capacity was available, to map out the conflict's dynamics and analyse data, to have a clearer picture of its humanitarian and security consequences, to understand local political claims and the war's social consequences for conflict-affected social groups, and to provide a clearer picture of its geopolitics. Indeed, digital technologies and approaches, though initially and widely viewed as promising, could be argued to have mainly augmented war-making in Syria rather than peacemaking (Al Khatib and Xynou 2015; British Council and Build Up 2016).

Such failures probably would not have been avoided with emergence of new digital technologies, big data, and AI-based solutions. Sufficient data already existed as did the methods of conflict prevention, peacekeeping, and peacemaking, all of which were undermined by the failure of multilateralism and the lack of international political will, in Syria and Ukraine as in so many recent cases where peacemaking has failed or become frozen. No new data, variables, or methods would have saved Syria or Ukraine's populations from war under these conditions. This failure has placed the legitimacy of international and civil society actors actually trying to reform the state, support human rights and democracy, and extend the international capacities for peacemaking via the existing international peace architecture frameworks for diplomacy, mediation, intervention, rights, and law, at great risk. In other words, so far at least, technological supplements for peacemaking and peacebuilding activities are immature and risk deflecting from their failures and limitations. They may displace the long-standing need to address substantive security, rights, and justice concerns in conflict-affected societies. The next step, therefore, in this research agenda would be to look at substantially scaling up digital peace capacities and methodologies so that they are commensurate – or more capable – than the related shifts that have occurred in international relations, and in war-making.

To summarize, the advent of digital, datafication, remote, and mobile technologies in the twenty-first century has clearly outflanked the military–industrial scale of the peace tools the UN developed in the twentieth century in the period after World War II. Global terrorism, insurgency, hybrid wars, surveillance capitalism, and enormous unmet sights claims from subaltern actors around the world are indicative of this huge gulf between international disorder (in the co-existing, contemporary liberal international and multipolar frameworks) and existing peace tools. This indicates that there is an ongoing structural change in the international system, a new stage in its development with enormous implications for peacemaking, peacekeeping, development, mediation, diplomacy, conflict resolution, and other related peace tools, as well as the way scholarship on peace is developed. Yet the digital additions to the practical and epistemological armoury of peacemaking, while perhaps promising, are in no way commensurate with the changes that have occurred in digital international relations. The latter are global, deep, macro-level changes, which are as yet little understood, while the digital augmentation of peace tools operates mainly in micro or meso terrains of international relations, with little impact on the structural problems of the international system. This gulf – as in the Ukraine war currently – means wars are emerging untreated, and for which the current sets of tools have little response (other than more war or minor ameliorations). The scale and capacity of digital peacemaking tools need to be commensurate with the changes that have emerged concurrently in the international system in this current digital epoch, an urgent task for which a start has been made, but progress is still far too limited.

References

Al Khatib, H. and Xynou, M. (2015). Syria's Digital Civil War, *Open Democracy*, 13 February. www.opendemocracy.net/en/opensecurity/syrias-digital-civil-war/.

Allan, D. (2020). The Minsk Conundrum: Western Policy and Russia's War in Eastern Ukraine, Chatham House Ukraine Forum. www.chathamhouse.org/2020/05/minsk-conundrum-western-policy-and-russias-war-eastern-ukraine-0/minsk-2-agreement.

Allan, D. (2020). The Minsk Conundrum: Western Policy and Russia's War in Eastern Ukraine, Chatham House Ukraine Forum. www.chathamhouse.org/2020/05/minsk-conundrum-western-policy-and-russias-war-eastern-ukraine-0/minsk-2-agreement.

Amnesty International. (2019). Laws Designed to Silence: The Global Crackdown on Civil Society Organisations. 21 February. www.amnesty.org/en/documents/act30/9647/2019/en/.

Aradau, C. (2017). Assembling (non)knowledge: Security, law and surveillance in a digital world. *International Political Sociology*, 11(4), 327–42.

Aradau, C., and Blanke, T. (2017). Politics of prediction: Security and the time/space of governmentality in the age of big data. *European Journal of Social Theory*, 20(3), 373–91.

Arendt, H. (1951). *The Origins of Totalitarianism*. San Diego, CA: Harcourt Brace.

Arimatsu, L. (2019). Silencing women in the digital age. *Cambridge International Law Journal*, 8(2), 187–217.

Avgerou, C. (2003). The link between ICT and economic growth in the discourse of development. In M. Korpela, R. Montealegre and A. Poulymenakou, eds. *Organizational Information Systems in the Context of Globalization*. Cham: Springer, pp. 373–86.

Badouard, R., Mabi, C., and Sire, G. (2016). Beyond 'points of control': Logics of digital governmentality. *Internet Policy Review*, 5(3), 1–13.

Bailard, C. S. (2015). Ethnic conflict goes mobile: Mobile technology's effect on the opportunities and motivations for violent collective action. *Journal of Peace Research*, 52(3), 323–37.

Bailliet, C. M. and Larsen, K. M. eds. (2015). *Promoting Peace through International Law*. Oxford: Oxford University Press.

Barbara, J. (2008). Rethinking neo-liberal state building: Building post-conflict development states. *Development in Practice*, 18(3), 307–18.

Barber, T. (2016). A Renewed Nationalism Is Stalking Europe, *Financial Times*, 11 July. www.ft.com/content/53fc4518-4520-11e6-9b66-0712b3873ae1.

BBC News. (2013). UN Starts Drone Surveillance in DR Congo, 3 December. www.bbc.com/news/world-africa-25197754.

Beaumont, P. (2010). The Afgooye Corridor: World Capital of Internally Displaced People, *Guardian*, 4 October. www.theguardian.com/global-devel opment/poverty-matters/2010/oct/04/somalia-afgooye-corridor-displaced-people.

Bell, C. and Pospisil, J. (2017). Navigating inclusion in transitions from conflict: The formalised political unsettlement. *Journal of International Development*, 29(5), 576–93.

Bellamy, A. (2019). *World Peace (And How We Can Achieve It)*. Oxford: Oxford University Press.

Belloni, R. (2020). *The Rise and Fall of Peacebuilding in the Balkans*. London: Palgrave Macmillan.

Betz, D. J. and Stevens, T. (2013). Analogical reasoning and cyber security. *Security Dialogue*, 44(2), 147–64.

Biebricher, T. (2020). Neoliberalism and authoritarianism. *Global Perspectives*, 1(1), 11872–992.

Boyd, D. and Crawford, K. (2012). Critical questions for big data. *Information, Communication & Society*, 15(5), 662–79.

British Council and Build Up. (2016). Innovative Peacebuilding in Syria: A Scoping Study of the Strategic Use of Technology to Build Peace in the Syrian Context. https://syria.britishcouncil.org/sites/default/files/peacetech_report_web_en.pdf.

Brunnhuber, S. (2018). How can blockchain technology helps us to finance SDGs?, Presentation at the World Association for Sustainable Development 16th International Annual Conference, 10–12 April. https://youtu.be/5pDti101f-Y.

Buzan, B. (2014). The logic and contradictions of 'peaceful rise/development' as China's grand strategy. *The Chinese Journal of International Politics*, 7(4), 381–420.

Buzan, B. and Lawson, G. (2013). The global transformation: The nineteenth century and the making of modern international relations. *International Studies Quarterly*, 57(3), 620–34.

Buzan, B. and Lawson. G. (2014). Capitalism and the emergent world order. *International Affairs*, 90(1), 71–91.

Castells, M. (2009). *Communication Power*. Oxford: Oxford University Press.

Chandler, D. (2014). Beyond neoliberalism: resilience, the new art of governing complexity. *Resilience*, 2(1), 47–63.

Chandler, D. (2014). *Resilience: The Governance of Complexity*. London: Routledge.

Chandler, D. (2018). *Ontopolitics in the Anthropocene*. London: Routledge.

Clark, J. D. and Themudo, N. S. (2006). Linking the web and the street: Internet-based 'dotcauses' and the 'anti-globalization' movement. *World Development*, 24(1), 50–74.

Clausen, M. and Albrecht, P. (2021). Interventions since the cold war: From statebuilding to stabilization, *International Affairs*, 97(4), 1203–20.

Connolly, W. (2017). *Facing the Planetary: Entangled Humanism and the Politics of Swarming*. Durham: Duke University Press.

Costantini, I. and Hanau Santini, R. H. (2022). Power mediators and the 'illiberal peace' momentum: Ending wars in Libya and Syria. *Third World Quarterly*, 43(1), 131–47.

Coward, M. (2017). Against network thinking: A critique of pathological sovereignty. *European Journal of International Relations*, 24(2), 443–63.

Cox, R. W. (1981). Social forces, states and world orders: Beyond international relations theory. *Millennium*, 10(2), 126–55.

Crutzen, P. J. (2002). Geology of mankind: The anthropocene. *Nature*, 415, 23.

de Oliveira, R. S. (2011). Illiberal peacebuilding in Angola. *The Journal of Modern African Studies*, 49(2), 287–314.

DeGooyer, S. Hunt, A., Maxwell, L. and Moyn, S. (2018). *The Right to Have Rights*. London: Verso.

Der Derian, J. (2001). *Virtuous War: Mapping the Military-Industrial-Media-Entertainment-Network*. Boulder: Westview Press.

Der Derian, J. (2013). From War 2.0 to quantum war: The superpositionality of global violence. *Australian Journal of International Affairs*, 67(5), 570–85.

Der Derian. J. (2019). A quantum of insecurity. *New Perspectives*, 27(2), 13–27.

Dorn, A.W. (2016). *Smart peacekeeping: Towards tech-enabled operations. Providing for peacekeeping No.13*. New York: International Peace Institute.

Doyle, M. (1983). Kant, liberal legacies, and foreign affairs. *Philosophy and Public Affairs*, 12(3), 205–35.

Dragu, T. and Lupu. Y. (2021). Digital authoritarianism and the future of human rights. *International Organization*, 75(4), 991–1017.

Duffield, M. (2010). Risk-management and the fortified aid compound: Everyday life in post-interventionary society. *Journal of Intervention and Statebuilding*, 4(4), 453–74.

Duffield, M. (2019) *Post-Humanitarianism*. Cambridge: Polity Press.

Dürbeck, G., Schaumann, C. and Sullivan, H.I. (2016). Human and non-human agencies in the anthropocene. *Ecozon@*, 6(1), 118–36.

Elden, S. (2011). *The Birth of Territory.* Chicago: University of Chicago Press.

Fairclough, N. (2013). Critical discourse analysis and critical policy studies. *Critical Policy Studies,* 7(2), 177–97.

Farrell, H. and Newman, A. L. (2019). Weaponized interdependence: How global economic networks shape state coercion. *International Security,* 44(1), 42–79.

Farrell, T. and Gordon, S. (2009). COIN machine: The british military in Afghanistan. *RUSI Journal,* 154(3), 18–25.

Finnemore, M. and Sikkink, K. (1998). International norm dynamics and political change. *International Organization,* 52(4), 887–917.

Fletcher, T. (2016). *Naked Diplomacy.* London: William Collins.

Fortna, V. P. (2008). *Does Peacekeeping Work? Shaping Belligerents' Choices after Civil War.* Princeton: Princeton University Press.

Foucault, M. (1982). The subject and power. *Critical Inquiry,* 8(4), 777–95.

Foucault, M. (1995) *Discipline and Punish: The Birth of the Prison,* Alan Sheridan (Translator), New York: Vintage.

Freedman, L. (1998). Britain and the revolution in military affairs. *Defense Analysis,* 14(1), 55–66.

Freedom House. (2017). Democracy in Crisis. https://freedomhouse.org/report/freedom-world/freedom-world-2018.

Freire, M. R. and Simão, L. (2021). Peace and security in the age of hybrid wars. In O. P. Richmond, and G Visoka, eds. *The Oxford Handbook of Peacebuilding, Statebuilding, and Peace Formation.* New York: Oxford University Press, pp. 400–13.

Fritsch, S. (2014). Conceptualizing the ambivalent role of technology in international relations: Between systemic change and continuity. In M. Mayer, M. Carpes and K. Knoblich, eds. *The Global Politics of Science and Technology* Vol. 1. Cham: Springer, pp. 115–38.

Fukuyama, F. (1988). The end of history, *The National Interest,* 16, 3–18.

Galtung, J. (1969). Violence, peace, and peace research. *Journal of Peace Research,* 6(3), 167–91.

Gaskell. J. R., Larrauri, H.P., Rieken, J., Ali, A. and Ritgerink, A. (2016). *Uses of Information and Communication Technologies (ICTs) for EU Conflict Prevention and Peacebuilding.* London: London School of Economics and Political Sciences and Build Up.

Gellner, E. (2006). *Nations and Nationalism,* 2nd ed. Oxford: Blackwell.

George, J. (1994). *Discourses of Global Politics: A Critical Introduction to International Relations.* Boulder, CO: Lynne Rienner.

Gilman, D. and Baker, L. (2014). *Humanitarianism in the Age of Cyberwarfare: Towards the Principled and Secure Use of Information in*

Humanitarian Emergencies. New York: UN Office for the Coordination of Humanitarian Affairs.

Gleditsch, K. S. (2019). An ever more violent world? *Political Studies Review*, 17(2), 99–114.

Gohdes, A. R. (2015). Pulling the plug: Network disruption and violence in civil conflict. *Journal of Peace Research*, 52(3), 352–67.

Goldstein, J. S. (2011). *Winning the War on War: The Decline of Armed Conflict Worldwide*. New York: Dutton.

Gonzalez-Vicente, R. (2020). The liberal peace fallacy: Violent neoliberalism and the temporal and spatial traps of state-based approaches to peace. *Territory, Politics, Governance*, 8(1), 100–16.

Graham, S. (1998). The end of geography or the explosion of place? Conceptualizing space, place and information technology. *Progress in Human Geography*, 22(2), 165–85.

Grose, P. (1996). *Continuing the Inquiry: The Council on Foreign Relations from 1921 to 1996*. New York: The Council on Foreign Relations.

Guo, W., Gleditsch, K. S., and Wilson, A. (2018). Retool AI to forecast and limit wars. *Nature*, 562, 331–3.

Habermas, J. (1989). *Between Facts and Norms: Contributions to a Discourse Theory of Law and Democracy*. Translated by William Rehng. Cambridge, MA: The MIT Press.

Haggard, S. and Kaufman, R. (2021). *Backsliding*. Cambridge: Cambridge University Press.

Harvey, D. (2005). *A Brief History of Neoliberalism*. Chicago: University of Chicago Center for International Studies.

Hassan, R. (2016). Analogue time, analogue people and the digital eclipsing of modern political time. In A. Hom, C. Mcintosh, A. Mckay and L. Stockdale, eds. Time, *Temporality and Global Politics*. London: E-International Relations.

Hassan, R. (2018). Digital, ethical, political: Network time and common responsibility. *New Media and Society*, 20(7), 2534–49.

Hassan, R. (2018). There isn't an app for that: Analogue and digital politics in the age of platform capitalism. *Media Theory*, 2(2), 1–28.

Hassan, R. (2021). Analogue ontology and digital disruption. *Educational Philosophy and Theory*, 53(4), 383–92.

Hattotuwa, S. (2004). Untying the Gordian Knot: ICT for Conflict Transformation and Peacebuilding. https://ict4peace.org/wp-content/uploads/2019/08/ICT4Peace-2004-Untying-The-Gordian-Knot.pdf.

Held, D. (2004). *Global Covenant: The Social Democratic Alternative to the Washington Consensus*. Cambridge: Polity Press.

Hellmüller, S. (2021). The challenge of forging consent to UN mediation in internationalized civil wars: The case of Syria. *International Negotiation*, 27(1), 103–30.

Hinnebusch, R. (2015). Globalization, democratization, and the Arab uprising: The international factor in MENA's failed democratization. *Democratization*, 22(2), 335–57.

Hinsley, F. H. (1963). *Power and the Pursuit of Peace*. Cambridge: Cambridge University Press.

Hirblinger, A. (2020). *Designing Digital Inclusion in Peacemaking: Summary of Findings*. Geneva: Graduate Institute for International and Development Studies.

Hirblinger. A. T. (2020). *Digital Inclusion in Mediated Peace Processes: How Technology Can Enhance Participation*, US Institute of Peace. www.usip .org/publications/2020/09/digital-inclusion-mediated-peace-processes-how-technology-can-enhance.

Hirblinger, A. T., Hansen, J. M., Hoelscher, K. et al. (2022). Digital peace-building: A framework for critical–reflexive engagement. *International Studies Perspectives*. https://doi.org/10.1093/isp/ekac015.

Hobsbawm, E. J. (1990). *Nations and Nationalism since 1780: Programme, Myth, Reality*, 2nd ed. Cambridge: Cambridge University Press.

Hoffman, D. (2007). *Conflict in the 21st Century: The Rise of Hybrid Wars*. Arlington, VA: Potomac Institute for Policy Studies.

Holbrooke, R. (1998). *To End a War*. New York: Random House.

Howard, P. H. (2015). *Pax Technica*. New Haven, CT: Yale University Press.

Hristov, J. (2016). *Paramilitarism and Neoliberalism: Violent Systems of Capital Accumulation in Colombia and Beyond*. Cambridge: Pluto Press.

Hughes, C. and Pupavac, V. (2005). Framing post-conflict societies: An analysis of the international pathologisation of Cambodia and the post-yugoslav states. *Third World Quarterly*, 26(6), 873–89.

Hunt, A. and Specht, D. (2019). Crowdsourced mapping in crisis zones: Collaboration, organisation and impact. *Journal of International Humanitarian Action*, 4(1), 1–11.

Hurrell, A. (2008). *On Global Order: Power, Values, and the Constitution of International Society*. Oxford: Oxford University Press.

Hurwitz, R. (2014). The play of states: Norms and security in cyberspace. American *Foreign Policy Interests*, 36(5), 322–31.

Imran, M., Meier, P., and Boersma, F. K. (2018). The use of social media for crisis management: A privacy by design approach. In K. Boersma and C. Fonio, eds. *Big data, Surveillance and Crisis Management*. London: Routledge, pp.19–37.

International Alert. (2020). *Can We Build Peace from a Distance? The Impact of COVID-19 on the Peacebuilding Sector.* Background Paper. London: International Alert.

Scholte, J. A. (2001). Civil Society and democracy in Global Governance, Centre for the Study of Globalization and Regionalisation, Working Paper No.65/01.

Jacobsen, K. L. (2015). *The Politics of Humanitarian Technology: Good Intentions, Unintended Consequences and Insecurity.* London: Routledge.

John Lewis Gaddis, J. L. (1986). The long peace: Elements of stability in the postwar international system. *International Security,* 10(4), 99–142.

Jones, B. and Marc, A. (2021). The New Geopolitics of Fragility: Russia, China, and the Mounting Challenge for Peacebuilding, Brookings Institute. www .brookings.edu/research/the-new-geopolitics-of-fragility-russia-china-and-the-mounting-challenge-for-peacebuilding/.

Juris, J. S. (2005). The new digital media and activist networking within anti-corporate globalization movements. *ANNALS: American Academy of Political and Social Science,* 597(1), 189–208.

Jütersonke, O., Kobayashi, K., Krause, K., and Yuan, X. (2021). Norm contestation and normative transformation in global peacebuilding order(s): The cases of China, Japan, and Russia. *International Studies Quarterly,* 65(4), 944–59.

Kaldor, M. (2003). The idea of global civil society. *International Affairs,* 79(3), 583–93.

Kaldor, M. and Kostovicova, D. (2021). Global civil society, peacebuilding and statebuilding. In O. P. Richmond and G. Visoka, eds. *The Oxford Handbook of Peacebuilding, Statebuilding and Peace Formation.* New York: Oxford University Press, pp. 328–40.

Karlsrud, J. (2014). Peacekeeping 4.0: Harnessing the potential of big data, social media and cyber technologies. In J. Kremer and B. Müller, eds. *Cyberspace and International Relations: Theory, Prospects and Challenges.* Cham: Springer, pp. 141–60.

Karlsrud, J. and Rosén, F. (2013). In the eye of the beholder? The UN and the use of drones to protect civilians. *Stability: International Journal of Security and Development,* 2(2), 1–10.

Keane, J. (1988). *Civil Society and the State: New European Perspectives.* Cambridge: Polity Press.

Keck, M. E. and Sikkink, K. (1998). *Activists Beyond Borders: Advocacy Networks in International Politics.* Ithaca: Cornell University Press.

Kennan, G. F. (1947). The sources of soviet conduct. *Foreign Affairs,* 25(4), 566–82.

Kennan, G. F. (1984). *American Diplomacy*. Chicago: University of Chicago Press.

Kennedy, P. (1987). *The Rise and Fall of the Great Powers: Economic Change and Military Conflict from 1500 to 2000*. New York: Vintage Books.

Keohane, R. O. and Nye, J. S. Jr. (1977). *Power and Interdependence: World Politics in Transition*. Boston, Little Brown Pub.

Knox, H. and Walford, A. (2016). Is There an Ontology to the Digital? Theorizing the Contemporary, Cultural Anthropology website, 24 March. https://culanth.org/fieldsights/818-is-there-an-ontology-to-the-digital.

Kobrin, K. (2020). Sliding into Isolation: Russia and the World, Open Democracy, 23 December. www.opendemocracy.net/en/odr/russia-isolation-kobrin/.

Kohn, M. (2013). Postcolonialism and global justice. *Journal of Global Ethics*, 9(2), 187–200.

Koopman, C. (2013). *Genealogy as Critique: Foucault and the Problems of Modernity*. Indianapolis, IN: Indiana University Press.

Krause, J. (2019). Stabilization and local conflicts: Communal and civil war in South Sudan. *Ethnopolitics*, 18(5), 478–93.

Kwet. M. (2019). Digital colonialism: US empire and the new imperialism in the Global South. *Race & Class*, 60(4), 3–26.

Landau, D. M. and Lehrs, L. (2022). Populist peacemaking: Trump's peace initiatives in the Middle East and the Balkans. *International Affairs*, 98(6), 2001–19.

Lapid, Y. (1989). The third debate: On the prospects of international theory in a post-positivist era. *International Studies Quarterly*, 33(3), 235–54.

Larrauri, H. P. and Kahl, A. (2013). Technology for peacebuilding. *Stability: International Journal of Security and Development*, 2(3), 1–15.

Larauri, H. P. and Meier, P. (2015). *Peacekeepers in the Sky: The Use of Unmanned Unarmed Aerial Vehicles for Peacekeeping*. New York: ICT4Peace Foundation.

Latour, B. (2005). *Reassembling the Social. An Introduction to the Actor-Network Theory*. Oxford: Oxford University Press.

Lawton, A. (2022). Alibaba Group president J. Michael Evans boasts at the World Economic Forum about the development of an 'individual carbon footprint tracker' to monitor what you buy, what you eat, and where/how you travel. 24 May. https://twitter.com/AndrewLawton/status/15290451887 64921856?s=20&t=SoLMEUo5YP9j-3SddE3dTw.

Leaning, J. and Meier, P. (2009). *The Untapped Potential of Information Communication Technology for Conflict Early Warning and Crisis Mapping*. Working Paper Series. Cambridge, MA: Harvard Humanitarian Initiative.

Lederach, J. P. (1995). *Preparing for Peace: Conflict Transformation Across Cultures*. Syracuse: Syracuse University Press.

Lederach, J. P. (1997). *Building Peace: Sustainable Reconciliation in Divided Societies*. Washington, DC: U.S. Institute of Peace.

Leroux-Martin, P. (2014). *Diplomatic Counterinsurgency: Lessons from Bosnia and Herzegovina*. Cambridge: Cambridge University Press.

Lewis, D., Heathershaw, J., and Megoran, N. (2018). Illiberal peace? Authoritarian modes of conflict management. *Cooperation and Conflict*, 53(4), 486–506.

Locke, J. (1988). *Two Treatises of Government*. ed. Peter Laslett. Cambridge: Cambridge University Press.

Loffredo, J. (2022). Pfizer CEO Albert Bourla explains Pfizer's new tech to Davos crowd: 'ingestible pills' – a pill with a tiny chip that send a wireless signal to relevant authorities when the pharmaceutical has been digested. 'Imagine the compliance', he says. 20 May. https://twitter.com/loffredojer emy/status/1527521228688445442?s=20&t=pHfhjKzu_0TMz6DpCy1yAg.

Loh, M. (2022). Canada says it will freeze the bank accounts of 'Freedom Convoy' truckers who continue their anti-vaccine mandate blockades, Business Insider, 15 February, www.businessinsider.com/trudeau-canada-freeze-bank-accounts-freedom-convoy-truckers-2022-2?op=1.

Mac Ginty, R. (2017). Peacekeeping and data. *International Peacekeeping*, 24(5), 695–705.

Mac Ginty, R. and Richmond, O. P. (2013). The local turn in peace building: A critical agenda for peace. *Third World Quarterly*, 34(5), 763–83.

Mancini, F. ed. (2013) *New Technology and the Prevention of Conflict*. New York: International Peace Institute.

Arias-Maldonado, M. (2013). Rethinking sustainability in the anthropocene. *Environmental Politics*, 22(3), 428–46.

Markland, A. (2022). Epistemic transformation at the margins: Resistance to digitalisation and datafication within global human rights advocacy. *Global Society*, 36(1),113–33.

Martin-Shields, C. P. and Bodanac, N. (2018). Peacekeeping's digital economy: The role of communication technologies in post-conflict economic growth. *International Peacekeeping*, 25(3), 420–45.

Massumi, B. (2002). *Parables for the Virtual: Movement, Affect, Sensation*. Durham, NC: Duke University Press.

Mazower, M. (2012). *Governing the World: The History of an Idea, 1815 to the Present*. London: Penguin.

Mazower, M. (2012). *Governing the World*. London: Penguin.

McCarthy, D. R. ed. (2017). *Technology and World Politics: An Introduction.* London: Routledge.

Meier, P. (2015). *Digital Humanitarians: How Big Data Is Changing the Face of Humanitarian Response.* London: Routledge.

Melucci, A. (1989). *Nomads of the Present: Social Movements and Individual Needs in Contemporary Society.* Philadelphia, PA: Temple University Press.

Merrin, W. (2019). *Digital War: A Critical Introduction.* London: Routledge.

Miklian, J. and Hoelscher, K. (2017). A new research approach for peace innovation. *Innovation and Development*, 8(2), 189–207.

Miller, E., Kishi, R., Raleigh, C., and Dowd, C. (2022). An agenda for addressing bias in conflict data. *Science Data*, 9, 593.

Milner, H. and Solstad, S. (2021). Technological change and the international system. *World Politics*, 73(3), 545–89.

Mishra, P. (2012). *From the Ruins of Empire: The Revolt Against the West and the Remaking of Asia.* London: Penguin.

Monroy-Hernández, A., Kiciman, E., Boyd, D. and Counts, S. (2012). Tweeting the drug war: Empowerment, intimidation and regulation in social media, Human Computer Interaction International Conference. www.microsoft .com/en-us/research/wp-content/uploads/2016/02/tweeting-war.pdf.

Monshipouri, M. and Mokhtari, S. (2016). The quest for human rights in the digital age. In M. Monshipouri, ed. *Information Politics, Protests and Human Rights in the Digital Age.* Cambridge: Cambridge University Press, pp.267–93.

Monshipouri, M., ed. (2016). *Politics, Protests and Human Rights in the Digital Age.* Cambridge: Cambridge University Press.

Monten, J. (2014). Intervention and state-building: Comparative lessons from Japan, Iraq, and Afghanistan. *The Annals of the American Academy of Political and Social Science*, 656(4), 173–91.

Morgenbesser, L. (2019) Cambodia's transition to hegemonic authoritarianism. *Journal of Democracy*, 30(1), 158–71.

Morozov, E. (2011). *The Net Delusion. How not to Liberate the World.* New York: Allen Lane.

Morrison, C. (2016) Engaging with local communities to prevent violence: What role for the ICTs?. Research Summary, Making all Voices Count. https://core.ac.uk/download/pdf/77037297.pdf.

Morsink, J. (1999). *The Universal Declaration of Human Rights: Origins, Drafting, and Intent.* Philadelphia, PA: University of Pennsylvania Press.

Morton, S. (2007). *Gayatri Spivak: Ethics, Subalternity and the Critique of Postcolonial Reason.* Cambridge: Polity Press.

Moyn, S. (2018). *Not Enough: Human Rights in and Unequal World.* Cambridge, MA: Harvard University Press.

Muller, L. P. (2015). *Cyber Security Capacity Building in Developing Countries: Challenge and Opportunities*. Oslo: Norwegian Institute of International Affairs.

Nagel, T. (2005). The problem of global justice. *Philosophy & Public Affairs*, 33(2), 113–47.

Negroponte, D. V. (2011). *Seeking Peace in El Salvador*. London: Palgrave.

Newman, E. and Richmond, O. P., eds. (2006). *Challenges to Peacebuilding: Managing Spoilers During Conflict Resolution*. Tokyo: UNU Press.

O'Neill, O. (2000). *Bounds of Justice*. Cambridge: Cambridge University Press.

Öniş, Z., and Kutlay, M. (2020). The new age of hybridity and clash of norms: China, BRICS, and challenges of global governance in a postliberal international order. *Alternatives*, 45(3), 123–42.

Ostrom, E. (1990). *Governing the Commons: The Evolution of Institutions for Collective Action*. Cambridge: Cambridge University Press.

Owen, T. (2015). *Disruptive Power: The Crisis of the State in the Digital Age*. Oxford: Oxford University Press.

Paine, T. (2000). *Rights of Man*. New York: Dover.

Paris, R. (2010). Saving liberal peacebuilding. *Review of International Studies*, 32(2), 337–65.

Paris, R. (2020). The right to dominate: How old ideas about sovereignty pose new challenges for world order. *International Organization*, 74(3), 453–89.

Peace Direct. (2020). Digital Pathways to Peace: Insights and Lessons from a Global Online Consultation. www.peacedirect.org/wp-content/uploads/2020/08/PD-LVP-Tech-Report.pdf.

PeaceTech Lab (2022) Sawa Shabab (Together Youth). Washington, DC: PeaceTech Lab. www.peacetechlab.org/sawa-shabab-radio.

Peters, B. (2016). Digital. In B. Peters, ed. *Digital Keywords: A Vocabulary of Information Society and Culture*. Princeton, NJ: Princeton University Press, pp. 93–108.

Piketty, T. (2014). *Capital in the Twenty-First Century*. Cambridge, MA: Belknap Press.

Pinker, S. (2011). *The Better Angels of Our Nature: Why Violence Has Declined*. New York: Viking.

Pogge, T. (2005). World poverty and human rights. *Ethics & International Affairs* 19(1), 1–7.

Pogodda, P. (2020). Revolutions and the liberal peace: Peacebuilding as counterrevolutionary practice?. *Cooperation and Conflict*, 55(3), 347–64.

Pogodda, S. and Richmond, O. P. (2015). Palestinian unity and everyday state formation: Subaltern 'ungovernmentality' versus elite interests. *Third World Quarterly*, 36(5), 890–907.

Pogodda, S., Richmond, O. P., and Visoka, G. (2022). Counter-peace: From isolated blockages in peace processes to systemic patterns. *Review of International Studies*, https://doi.org/10.1017/S0260210522000377.

Polanyi, K. (1944). *The Great Transformation*. New York: Farrar & Rinehart.

Pugh, M. (2004). Peacekeeping and critical theory. *International Peacekeeping*, 11(1), 39–58.

Pugh, M. (2005). The political economy of peacebuilding: A critical theory perspective. *International Journal of Peace Studies*, 10(2), 23–42.

Qin, Y. (2018). A relational theory of world politics. *International Studies Review*, 18(1), 33–47.

Ratelle, J. and Souleimanov, E. A. (2016). A perfect counterinsurgency? Making sense of Moscow's policy of chechenisation. *Europe-Asia Studies*, 68(8), 1287–314.

Rawls, J. (1993). The law of peoples. *Critical Inquiry*, 20(1), 36–68.

Read, R., Taithe, B., and Mac Ginty, R. (2016). Data hubris? Humanitarian information systems and the mirage of technology. *Third World Quarterly*, 37(8), 1314–31.

Richmond, O. O. and Tellidis, I. (2020). Analogue crisis, digital renewal? Current dilemmas of peacebuilding. *Globalisations*, 17(6), 935–52.

Richmond, O. P. (2005). *The Transformation of Peace*. London: Palgrave.

Richmond, O. P. (2011). *A Post-Liberal Peace*. London: Routledge.

Richmond, O. P. (2014). *Failed Statebuilding: Intervention, the State, and the Dynamics of Peace Formation*. New Haven, CT: Yale University Press.

Richmond, O. P. (2016). *Peace Formation and Political Order in Conflict Affected Societies*. New York: Oxford University Press.

Richmond, O. P. (2017). The paradox of peace and power: Contamination or enablement? *International Politics*, 54(5), 637–58.

Richmond, O. P. (2020). Interventionary order and its methodologies: The relationship between peace and intervention. *Third World Quarterly*, 41(2), 207–27.

Richmond, O. P. (2020). Peace in analogue/ digital international relations. *Global Change, Peace & Security*, 32(3), 317–36.

Richmond, O. P. (2020). *Peace in International Relations*, 2nd ed. London: Routledge.

Richmond, O. P. (2021). Towards a peace with global justice? The struggle within the international peace architecture. *Asian International Studies Review*, 22(1), 36–64.

Richmond, O. P. (2021). What is an emancipatory peace. *Journal of International Political Theory*, 18(2), 124–47.

Richmond, O. P. (2022). *The Grand Design: The Evolution of International Peace Architecture*. New York: Oxford University Press.

Richmond, O. P. and Franks, J. (2008). *Liberal Peace Transitions*. Edinburgh: Edinburgh University Press.

Richmond, O. P. and Pogodda, S. eds. (2016). *Post-Liberal Peace Transitions*. Edinburgh: Edinburgh University Press.

Richmond, O. P. and Sandra Pogodda, S. (2016). Introduction: The contradictions of peace, international architecture, the state, and local agency. In O. P. Richmond and S. Pogodda, eds. *Post-Liberal Peace Transitions: Between Peace Formation and State Formation*. Edinburgh: Edinburgh University Press, pp. 1–26.

Richmond, O. P. and Visoka, G. (2021a). Peace-making: New technologies are no panacea. *Nature*, 590, 389.

Richmond, O. P. and Visoka, G. eds. (2021b). *The Oxford Handbook of Peacebuilding, Statebuilding, and Peace Formation*. New York: Oxford University Press.

Richmond, O. P. and Visoka, G. eds. (2022). *The Palgrave Encyclopedia of Peace and Conflict Studies*. Cham: Palgrave Macmillan.

Richmond, O. P., Mac Ginty, R., Pogodda, S., and Visoka, G. (2021). Power or peace? Restoration or emancipation through peace processes. *Peacebuilding*, 9(3), 243–57.

Richmond, O. P., Pogodda, S., and Ramovic, J. eds. (2016). *The Palgrave Handbook of Disciplinary and Regional Approaches to Peace*. Basingstoke: Palgrave Macmillan.

Richterich. A. (2018). *The Big Data Agenda: Data Ethics and Critical Data Studies*. London: University of Westminster Press.

Risse, M. (2005). Do we owe the global poor assistance or rectification? *Ethics & International Affairs*, 19(1), 9–18.

Rist, G. (2003). *The History of Development: From Western Origins to Global Faith*. London: Zed Books.

Roberts, S., Snee, H., Hine, C., Morey, Y., and Watson, H. eds. (2016). *Digital Methods for Social Science: An Interdisciplinary Guide to Research Innovation*. London: Palgrave.

Robinson, D. (2008). Analog. In M. Fuller, ed. *Software Studies: A Lexicon*, edited by Matthew Fuller. Cambridge, MA: The MIT Press, pp. 21–31.

Rød, E. G. and Weidmann, N. B. (2015). Empowering activists or autocrats? The internet in authoritarian regimes. *Journal of Peace Research*, 52(3), 338–51.

Rousseau, J. J. (1978). *On the Social Contract*, translated by Judith R Masters. New York: St Martin's Press.

Rush Doshi, R. (2021). *The Long Game: China's Grand Strategy to Displace American Order*. Oxford: Oxford University Press.

Sandvik, K. B., Jumbert, M.G., Karlsrud, J., and Kaufmann, M. (2014). Humanitarian technology: A critical research agenda. *International Review of the Red Cross*, 96(893), 219–42.

Schia, N. N. (2018). The cyber frontier and digital pitfalls in the global south. *Third World Quarterly*, 39(5), 821–37.

Schirch, L. (2020). 25 Spheres of Digital Peacebuilding and PeaceTech. Toda Peace Institute and Alliance for Peacebuilding, https://toda.org/assets/files/resources/policy-briefs/t-pb-93_lisa-schirch.pdf.

Scholvin, S. and Wigell, M. (2018). Power politics by economic means: Geoeconomics as an analytical approach and foreign policy practice. *Comparative Strategy*, 37(1), 73–84.

Schuler, I. (2008). SMS as a tool in election observation. *Innovations: Technology, Governance, Globalization*, 3(2), 143–57.

Shackelford, S. J. (2014). *Managing Cyber Attacks in International Law, Business, and Relations: In Search of Cyber Peace*. Cambridge: Cambridge University Press.

Shilliam, R. ed. (2010). *International Relations and Non-Western Thought*. London: Routledge.

Simmons, B. (2011). International studies in the global information Age. *International Studies Quarterly*, 55(3), 589–99.

Slaughter, A. (2004). Sovereignty and power in networked world order. *Stanford Journal of International Law*, 40(2), 283–328.

Smetana, M. and Ludvik, J. (2018). Between war and peace: A dynamic reconceptualization of 'frozen conflicts'. *Asia Europe Journal*, 17(1), 1–14.

Spykman, N. J. (1994). *The Geography of the Peace*. San Diego, CA: Harcourt, Brace.

Stauffacher, D., Weekes, B., Gasser, U Maclay, C. and Best, M. (2011). *Peacebuilding in the Information Age: Sifting Hype from Reality*. New York: ICT4Peace Foundation.

Stauffacher, D., Drake, W., and Currion, P. (2005). *Information and Communication Technology for Peace: The Role of ICT in Preventing, Responding to and Recovering from Conflict*. New York: United Nations ICT Task Force.

Stedman, S. J. (1997). Spoiler problems in peace processes. *International Security*, 22(2), 5–53.

Steffen, W., Grinevald, J., Crutzen, P. and McNeill, J. (2011). The anthropocene: Conceptual and historical perspectives. *Philosophical Transactions of the Royal Society*, 369(1938), 842–67.

Stent, A. (2022). The West vs. the Rest: Welcome to the 21st-century Cold War, Foreign Policy, 2 May. https://foreignpolicy.com/2022/05/02/ukraine-russia-war-un-vote-condemn-global-response/.

Sterne, J. (2016). Analog. In B. Peters, ed. Digital Keywords: A Vocabulary of Information Society and Culture. Princeton, NJ: Princeton University Press, pp. 31–44.

Strasheim, J. and Bogati, S. (2021). A challenge to the liberal peace? EU peacebuilding faces China in Nepal. *European Review of International Studies*, 8(3), 353–81.

Stuenkel, O. (2015). *The BRICS and the Future of Global Order*. Lanham, MA: Lexington Books.

Subedi, D. B. (2021). Rethinking peacebuilding in the age of populism. *Peace Review*, 33(4), 495–505.

Subedi. D. B. (2022) The emergence of populist nationalism and 'illiberal' peacebuilding in Sri Lanka. *Asian Studies Review*, 46(2), 272–92.

Sylvester, C. (2002). *Feminist International Relations: An Unfinished Journey*. Cambridge: Cambridge University Press.

Sylvester, C. (2011). The forum: Emotion and the feminist IR researcher. *International Studies Review*, 13(4), 687–708.

Tadjbakhsh, S. and Chenoy, A. M. (2006). *Human Security: Concepts and Implications*. London: Routledge.

Tainter, J. A. (1988). *The Collapse of Complex Societies*. Cambridge: Cambridge University Press.

Tardy, T. (2012). *Emerging Powers and Peacekeeping: An Unlikely Normative Clash, Policy Paper 2012/13*. Geneva: Geneva Centre for Security Policy.

Tellidis, I. and Kappler, S. (2016) Information and communication technologies in peacebuilding: Implications, opportunities and challenges. *Cooperation and Conflict*, 51(1),75–93.

Thaler, R. H. and Sunstein, C. R. (2008). *Nudge: Improving Decisions about Health, Wealth, and Happiness*. New Haven, CT: Yale University Press.

The Economist. (2016). The New Nationalism, 19 November. www.economist.com/leaders/2016/11/19/the-new-nationalism.

The Economist. (2018). Technology and its Discontents, 16 April. www.economist.com/open-future/2018/04/16/technology-and-its-discontents.

Tikk, E. (2018). *The Year that Cyber Peace Became Non-binding*. New York: ICT for Peace Foundation.

Tilly, C. (1990). *Coercion, Capital, and European States, AD 990–1990*. London: Blackwell.

`UN (2013) *Seoul Framework for and Commitment to Open and Secure Cyberspace*. www.un.org/disarmament/wp-content/uploads/2019/10/

ENCLOSED-Seoul-Framework-for-and-Commitment-to-an-Open-and-Secure-Cyberspace.pdf.

UN. (2015a). *Uniting our Strengths for Peace – Politics, Partnerships, and People: Report of the High-Level Independent Panel on United Nations Peace Operations*, UN Doc. A/70/95–S/2015/446, 17 June.

UN. (2015b). *Report of the Group of Governmental Experts on Developments in the Field of Information and Telecommunications in the Context of International Security*, UN Doc. A/70/174, 22 July.

UN. (2015c). *Performance Peacekeeping: Final Report of the Expert Panel on Technology and Innovation in UN Peacekeeping*. https://peacekeeping.un .org/en/final-report-of-expert-panel-technology-and-innovation-un-peacekeeping.

UN. (2018). High-level Meeting on Efforts Undertaken and Opportunities to Strengthen the United Nations' Work on Peacebuilding and Sustaining Peace, 24–25 April. www.un.org/pga/72/wp-content/uploads/sites/51/2018/05/ Summary-HLM-on-Peacebuilding-and-Sustaining-Peace.pdf.

UN. (2021). *UN Strategy for the Digital Transformation of UN Peacekeeping*. https://peacekeeping.un.org/sites/default/files/strategy-for-the-digital-trans formation-of-un-peacekeeping_en_final-01_15-08-2021_final.pdf.

UN Department of Peace Operations. (2021). *Strategy for the Digital Transformation of UN Peacekeeping*. New York: UN.

UN Development Program. (2017). *Spark, Scale, Sustain: Innovation for the Sustainable Development Goals*. New York: UNDP.

UN General Assembly. (2020). State of global peace and security in line with the central mandates contained in the Charter of the United Nations: Report of the Secretary-General, UN Doc. A/74/786, 6 April.

UN General Assembly and UN Security Council. (2015). Report of the high-level independent panel on peace operations on united our strengths for peace: Politics, partnership, and people, UN Doc. A/70/95-s/2001/446, 17 June.

UN General Assembly. (1950). Uniting for peace, UN Doc. A/RES/377(V), 3 November.

UN General Assembly. (2013). Format and organizational aspects of the high-level political forum on sustainable development, UN Doc.67/290 (2013), 12 July.

UN General Assembly. (2016). Review of the United Nations peacebuilding architecture, UN Doc. A/RES/70/262, 12 May.

UN Human Rights Council. (2021). Possible impacts, opportunities and challenges of new and emerging digital technologies with regard to the promotion and protection of human rights, UN Doc A/HRC/47/52, 19 May.

UN Human Security Unit. (2006). *UN Human Security Handbook*. New York: UN Human Security Unit.

UN News Center. (2013). UN peacekeeping mission in Mali increasingly possible, says top official, 6 February. www.un.org/apps/news/story.asp? NewsID=44087.

UN Secretary-General (2014) Technology must be used in making peacekeeping more safe, cost-effective, UN Doc. SG/SM/15929-SC/11435-PKO/411, 11 June. https://press.un.org/en/2014/sgsm15929.doc.htm.

UN Secretary-General. (2018). Report of the secretary-general, 'Peacebuilding and sustaining peace', UN Doc. A/72/707–S/2018/43, 18 January.

UN Secretary-General. (2020). State of global peace and security in line with the central mandates contained in the Charter of the United Nations, UN Doc. A/74/786, 6 April.

UN Security Council. (2006). Resolution 1706, UN Doc. S/RES/1706, 31 August.

UN Security Council. (2016). Resolution 2282, UN Doc. S/RES/2282, 27 April.

UN Security Council. (2021). 'Strategy for the Digital Transformation of UN Peacekeeping', New York, 18 August 18. https://peacekeeping.un.org/en/strategy-digital-transformation-of-un-peacekeeping.

Virilio, P. (2002). *Desert Screen: War at the Speed of Light*. London: Continuum.

Visoka, G. (2012). Three levels of hybridisation practices in post-conflict Kosovo. *Journal of Peacebuilding & Development*, 7(2), 23–36.

Visoka, G. (2016). Arrested truth: Transitional justice and the politics of remembrance in Kosovo. *Journal of Human Rights Practice*, 8(1), 62–80.

Visoka, G. (2016). *Peace Figuration After International Intervention: Interventions, Events and Consequences of Liberal Peacebuilding*. London: Routledge.

Visoka, G. (2017). *Shaping Peace in Kosovo: The Politics of Peacebuilding and Statehood*. Basingstoke: Palgrave Macmillan.

Visoka, G. (2019). Critique and alternativity in international relations. *International Studies Review*, 21(4), 678–704.

Visoka, G. and Lemay-Hébert, N. (2022). *Normalization in World Politics*. Ann Arbor: The University of Michigan Press.

Visoka, G. and Richmond, O. P. (2017). After liberal peace? From failed statebuilding to an emancipatory peace in Kosovo. *International Studies Perspectives*, 18(1), 110–29.

von Billerbeck, S. and Tansey, O. (2019). Enabling autocracy? Peacebuilding and post-conflict authoritarianism in the Democratic Republic of Congo. *European Journal of International Relations*, 25(3), 698–722.

Walker, R. B. J. (1993). *Inside/outside: International Relations as Political Theory*. Cambridge: Cambridge University Press.

Wallensteen, P. (2015). *Quality Peace: Strategic Peacebuilding and World Order*. Oxford: Oxford University of Press.

Warren, T. C. (2015). Explosive connections? Mass media, social media and the geography of collective violence in African states. *Journal of Peace Research*, 52(3), 297–311.

Weber, C. (2004) *International Relations Theory. A Critical Introduction*, 2nd ed. London: Routledge.

Welch, J., Halford, S., and Weal, M. (2015). Conceptualising the web for post-conflict governance building. *Peacebuilding*, 3(1), 58–74.

Wilden, A. (1980). *System and Structure: Essays in Communication and Exchange*. London: Tavistock.

Williams, P. (2005). Critical security studies. In A. Bellamy ed. *International Society and Its Critics*. Oxford: Oxford University Press, pp. 135–49.

Woodward, S. (2017). *The Ideology of Failed States*. Cambridge: Cambridge University Press.

World Food Programme. (2017). What Is 'Blockchain' and How Is It Connected to Fighting Hunger, 6 March. https://insight.wfp.org/what-is-blockchain-and-how-is-it-connected-to-fighting-hunger-7f1b42da9fe.

World Identity Network. (2017). World Identity Network and United Nations Team Up to Launch Innovative Blockchain Pilot to Help Prevent Child Trafficking, 10 November. www.prnewswire.com/newsreleases/world-identity-network-and-united-nations-team-up-to-launch-innovative-block chain-pilot-tohelp-prevent-child-trafficking-300553921.html.

Zartman, I. W. and Rasmussen, J. L. eds. (1997). *Peacemaking in International Conflict: Methods and Techniques*. Washington, DC: United States Institute of Peace Press.

Zheng, C. and Hang, Y. (2020). China and Russia in R2P debates at the UN security council. *International Affairs*, 96(3), 787–805.

Zuboff, S. (2019a). Surveillance capitalism and the challenge of collective action. *New Labor Forum*, 28(1), 10–29.

Zuboff, S. (2019b). *The Age of Surveillance Capitalism*. London: Profile.

Cambridge Elements $\equiv$

International Relations

Series Editors

Jon C. W. Pevehouse
University of Wisconsin–Madison

Jon C. W. Pevehouse is the Vilas Distinguished Achievement Professor of Political Science at the University of Wisconsin–Madison. He has published numerous books and articles in IR in the fields of international political economy, international organizations, foreign policy analysis, and political methodology. He is a former editor of the leading IR field journal, International Organization.

Tanja A. Börzel
Freie Universität Berlin

Tanja A. Börzel is the Professor of political science and holds the Chair for European Integration at the Otto-Suhr-Institute for Political Science, Freie Universität Berlin. She holds a PhD from the European University Institute, Florence, Italy. She is coordinator of the Research College "The Transformative Power of Europe," as well as the FP7-Collaborative Project "Maximizing the Enlargement Capacity of the European Union" and the H2020 Collaborative Project "The EU and Eastern Partnership Countries: An Inside-Out Analysis and Strategic Assessment." She directs the Jean Monnet Center of Excellence "Europe and its Citizens."

Edward D. Mansfield
University of Pennsylvania

Edward D. Mansfield is the Hum Rosen Professor of Political Science, University of Pennsylvania. He has published well over 100 books and articles in the area of international political economy, international security, and international organizations. He is Director of the Christopher H. Browne Center for International Politics at the University of Pennsylvania and former program co-chair of the American Political Science Association.

Editorial Team

About the series

The Cambridge Elements Series in International Relations publishes original research on key topics in the field. The series includes manuscripts addressing international security, international political economy, international organizations, and international relations.

Cambridge Elements ⚌

International Relations

Elements in the Series

Weak States at Global Climate Negotiations
Federica Genovese

Social Media and International Relations
Sarah Kreps

Across Type, Time and Space: American Grand Strategy in Comparative Perspective
Peter Dombrowski and Simon Reich

Moral Psychology, Neuroscience, and International Norms
Richard Price and Kathryn Sikkink

Contestations of the Liberal International Order
Fredrik Söderbaum, Kilian Spandler, Agnese Pacciardi

Domestic Interests, Democracy, and Foreign Policy Change
Brett Ashley Leeds, Michaela Mattes

Token Forces: How Tiny Troop Deployments Became Ubiquitous in UN Peacekeeping
Katharina P. Coleman, Xiaojun Li

Peace in Digital International Relations
Oliver P. Richmond, Gëzim Visoka, Ioannis Tellidis

A full series listing is available at: www.cambridge.org/EIR